Joan Wyndham

has led a rich and varied life since 1945, including opening Oxford's first espresso bar, running a hippy restaurant in London's Portobello Road, cooking at major pop festivals and catering for the actors at the Royal Court Theatre. She has also worked in Fleet Street on women's magazines, and as a food and wine critic in London and New York.

She is married with two daughters and lives in London.

JOAN WYNDHAM

Love is Blue

A Wartime Diary

Flamingo
An Imprint of HarperCollinsPublishers

Flamingo
An Imprint of HarperCollins*Publishers,*
77–85 Fulham Palace Road,
Hammersmith, London W6 8JB

Published by Flamingo 1987
9 8 7 6 5 4 3

First published in Great Britain by
William Heinemann Ltd 1986

The Author asserts the moral right to
be identified as the author of this work

ISBN 0 00 654201 8

Set in Bembo

Printed in Great Britain by
HarperCollinsManufacturing Glasgow

BOOK I

Sunday, 6th April 1941

The long, harrowing weeks of training are over and we are now
fully-fledged Filter Room Plotters, ready to keep track of anything
that flies from a wild goose to a Heinkel.

Up at crack of dawn, we packed our duffel bags – (Hitler
invades Greece, announced somebody's wireless) – and set off
gloomily for our new home, Preston, apparently the worst posting
you can get apart from Stornaway! Luckily I'm going with my
three best pals, Gussy, Pandora and Oscarine.

Our first view from the train windows didn't exactly cheer us
up – grey lines of brick houses, cobbled streets, a pall of smoke
from factory chimneys and a thundery sky. It was early evening
and already it was growing dark.

As we lugged our duffel bags across to the truck we were aware
of a strong reek of fish and chips. Leering old women with lank
grey hair were tottering along in clogs and shawls over the damp,
greasy cobbles, and most of the younger women seemed to be in the
family way. Some of the children had pink-eye, or rickets, or
were going bald, and we saw a lot of men who were crippled. We
began to feel more and more apprehensive.

About five miles outside of Preston the truck stopped before
what appeared to be the half-finished skeleton of a house. Surely
this couldn't be it? It was. Gussy, Pandora, Oscarine and self
staggered out, lugging our kit bags, and sat wearily down on the

bare metal bedsteads. Through cracks in the plaster an icy wind whistled around a large, bare room containing twenty beds, with metal lockers beside them.

'Oh, where we are is Hell, and where Hell is, there must we ever be!' quoted Oscarine, always the scholar – she is mad about Marlowe.

Gussy's fair curls were hanging down in wisps around her miserable little face; even the queenly Pandora, usually endowed with British phlegm, seemed a little dismayed.

None of the rooms seemed to have any doors nor the lavatories any paper nor the lavatory doors any locks, and the mattresses were bags stuffed with straw – great ears of corn sticking out right and left.

Gussy and I went gloomily up to the bathroom to wash, and a WAAF tore in, sat herself down on the WC and began to pee.

'What's this place like?' we asked.

'Lousy as hell,' she replied, wiping herself with a large sheet of newspaper. 'Just you wait and see!'

Hardly had she left when a peroxide blonde, nude except for a pair of soiled blue satin drawers, lurched in and began to retch into the basin.

'My God, I'm bloody drunk!' she said, rather unnecessarily.

Gussy and I took one look and fled.

Downstairs our sergeant was dishing out mugs of watery cocoa and spam sandwiches. Apparently it was too late for us to march up to the mess hall for supper, so we sat on the edge of our beds and clasped freezing hands around our mugs. In spite of our despair we felt happy that at least we were still together. Oscarine was my best friend at training camp. She was called Oscarine because her mother started having her during a matinée of *The Importance of Being Earnest*, but we usually call her Oscar. I think she is one of the prettiest girls I have ever seen. Soft dark hair falling forward over her cheeks, blue smudges under her almond eyes, and small wire spectacles which she wears on the end of her nose for reading, which she does all the time – mainly very highbrow things like Thomas Mann and Jung. I passionately admire her thin, keen, rather lesbian appearance, so unlike my own squashy femininity.

Gussy is gorgeous in quite a different way, a sort of blonde nymphomaniac with totally round, blue-grey eyes which make her look rather innocent. She walks in a very sexy way, leaning back from the hips as if offering herself to some invisible lover. She once told Oscar that her whole body was one vast erogenous zone. We looked this up, and are very jealous.

Pandora is one of those tall beautiful repressed girls who come from a good Catholic family – her mama is Lady Wynn-Waterlow. She has a rather handsome face, like a thoroughbred horse – high cheekbones, slightly reddened, and piercing grey eyes. I think being in the WAAFs is doing her a power of good, loosening her up and making her more human.

That night it was freezing cold and we all slept in our underclothes – except, that is, for Pandora, who changed into her oyster-grey silk pyjamas. She kept her pearls on too, because she says real pearls die if you take them off for too long.

I lay shivering in bed, thinking of my lost studio in Chelsea, so warm and cheery with the oil stove, and Rupert playing his guitar. I must remember to buy a hot water bottle tomorrow.

Monday, 7th

Our first day. Morning transport has apparently been cancelled so we have to get up at a quarter to six and walk a mile in the dark in order to have breakfast up at the main mess. Luckily there is a small electric ring in our quarters where we can do brew-ups. Also, just opposite, a wonderful cake shop selling meat pies, apple tarts, ice cream and licorice allsorts. We take them home and wash them down with gallons of strong tea.

After breakfast the rain stopped, so we were hauled out for PT by a ferocious Irish sergeant. By the time we had left-turned instead of right for the umpteenth time he was leaning weakly against the wall wiping imaginary tears from his eyes.

'My gawd, you 'orrible lot of wet sacks,' he groaned wearily, 'jumping over the puddles like a troop of little dancing dawls – *go through 'em!*'

'I don't think I can take much more of this,' Gussy said, as we changed our wet stockings back in the hut, 'there must be some way of getting out of here.'

'Not for ages,' I said, 'once you're sent to a Filter Headquarters as a plotter you're stuck for months – maybe years – until you can wangle some sort of posting.'

'There is one way out,' Pandora said. 'You become an officer. It's money for jam, you're waited on hand and foot, you live in a private hotel and never do a stroke of work. All we've got to do is catch the eye of one of the top brass and persuade him we are both clever and ladylike – actually it's *more* important to be ladylike.'

The day dragged on. We had a short break for lunch, tramping a mile uphill again for tinned pilchards on greasy fried bread. Over sour plums and watery custard we continued our escape plans.

'Sex,' Gussy said, 'that's what it all boils down to. Forget about being clever and ladylike, just grab yourself an officer, preferably a high-up one, and get to work on him.'

'Well, it'll have to be you,' we chorused and after that the conversation deteriorated into talking about sex.

Gussy, it seems, is one of those irritating girls who can have an orgasm simply by crossing her legs. Lucky old her. We, on the other hand, have found men, so far, a great disappointment. 'I mean it's so boring,' Oscar complained, 'they just lie on top of you, and make a few rather repetitive movements, and just as you're getting interested it all stops!'

I said it was just like that with Rupert. Sometimes I'd get excited when we weren't – you know – doing it, but when we were it was a dead loss. 'Mind you,' I went on, 'Rupert's the only man I've ever had, so perhaps there are better ones.'

'I've had three,' Oscar said gloomily, 'and each one was worse than the last.'

So it looks like Gussy is unanimously elected to do the grabbing. The choice of men here is not brilliant. Officers at Fighter Headquarters are not dashing pilots, they are usually admin, or if they *are* pilots, they are burnt-out cases with nervous tics and alcohol problems. It's not at all like the thrilling life WAAFs seem to have in films – 'Come in, Foxtrot Oscar,' and so on.

Tuesday, midnight

We are now on night duty. The underground Filter Room is huge and hectic, like a newspaper office in an American movie. You sit at an enormous table with a map of the area divided into squares, and wear headphones connecting you to the radar stations. They give you the height, position and numbers of the planes, and you plot their course on the map.

Upstairs in the gallery are fighter and bomber command officers, Fleet Air Arm people and liaison officers. Their job is to ring up their squadrons who then go and shoot down the enemy – or not, as the case may be.

Looking down from the officers' gallery, you would simply see a huge mass of writhing, heaving bottoms, everybody crawling on the table and knocking their neighbour out of the way. You seem to need an extra brain and four pairs of hands, not to mention an electronic body, as you hurl yourself across trying to get your plots down. We sweat terribly, and the earphones make our ears sore.

We also have to constantly harry the radio ops for fixes, they curse us back, the officers curse everybody and the scientific observers run around in small circles looking harassed. These are all young professors who stutter slightly, in grey flannels and brown sports coats. They usually have beautiful hands, and wear glasses.

The only other people upstairs are called Tellers. Every plotter's ambition is to be a Teller because you get to sit upstairs with the officers and are asked to bottle parties.

Sometimes you get long periods of doing nothing, and then you go in for something called 'binding'. This is an RAF expression meaning long, facetious chats over the wire with some filthy bounder in North Wales or Ireland – i.e. 'What's your name? Where do you come from? Chelsea eh? Coo-er! Bet you're hot stuff, have you got a beard? Hah hah! How much do you weigh, how big are your feet?' 'Shut up and let me get on with my knitting!'

This remark was a mistake as now they all think I'm in the family way – the dirty binders! Luckily a hostile aircraft usually crops up before they can get too obscene, and glues them to the cathode-ray tube again.

It's quiet so I'm writing this at the table. Have to be careful as the officers in the gallery have a habit of reading your letters through field-glasses.

The chief among these is our God, Massingham, a magnetic pilot-officer who simply reeks of allure. His reputation is so bad that any girl who dates him automatically asks for a sleeping-out pass. He is lean, dark and slightly sinister with a sardonic smile. He doesn't talk in a normal way, but says things like, 'There's bags of stuff in Robert Nuts, so stop binding and get me the gen, *now*!' We have decided he is It – the one Gussy is to work on, thus combining business with pleasure. All the girls fight like mad after Watch for the privilege of disinfecting his head-set.

It's 4 a.m. now and I feel like hell. My eyes keep closing and my head nodding. I'm trying to invent a technique of sleeping with my eyes open to fool the supervisors, but unfortunately I can't be sure that I am not dreaming they are open. Just my luck it's a busy night. A rumour has filtered down from the gallery, via our supervisor, that Coventry has bought it in a big way. Flight thinks they may have got the cathedral, the dirty buggers!

We are lucky to get even three hours sleep on truckle-beds, two to a mattress, head to foot! The grey blankets smell hauntingly of their previous occupants' feet, and it's our firm belief that they are never washed from one week to the next. Nevertheless these hours of rest are like paradise to us.

At the other end of our sleeping quarters is a long trestle table, laden with currant buns, Eccles cakes and meatpaste sandwiches, dry and curling at the edges. There is also a tea urn for our parched throats.

When the night comes to an end we still have to scrub out the whole Filter Room on our hands and knees, before we can stagger home to our beds. Per Ardua ad effing Astra and no mistake!

Wednesday

A new horror! Not only does the hay in our pillowcases stick in our ears at night, it also harbours fleas, and there are bedbugs in the blankets.

This morning I caught a huge flea and put him in a glass of water. The blankets have all gone to be fumigated. The bugs are red and as large as my thumbnail and their bites are torture. They well up into large blisters and then break. We also have nits in our hair. Pandora's is full of large ones that walk about. She is being treated, and having some of her hair cut away. I haven't caught them yet. We spend hours going through each other's scalps like monkeys.

Almost all the men over us who are not officers are communists and sadistic beasts. The worst is Flight Sergeant Hawkins, who looks like a vicious, criminal snake with a sniff that puckers up one side of his face — a trick he uses to great effect. To relieve our feelings we go in for orgies of hate — it's just like being back at school. We don't seem like adults at all, just a lot of silly schoolgirls without much intelligence, evading rules and talking about men. I must get out of here before I suffer brain damage.

We are also perpetually and clamorously hungry. Our main interest in life is food — we track around scouring the town for cheap grub. Our best bet is to take a penny platform ticket and go to the Free Forces Canteen, where if you fight your way through the hordes of sailors and tommies you can eat your fill for nothing, *and* stuff your kit-bag into the bargain.

Monday, 14th

Back on day duty and getting up at six. No time to traipse up for breakfast so we collect things the night before. The result is often poisonous and bizarre, as for instance this morning — plum cake, cheese sandwiches, pork pie and chocolate biscuits, washed down with Eno's!

The bugs are much better now, but they still don't give us any

Jeyes paper in the lavatory. I have worked my way steadily through a whole copy of Jung's *Psychology of the Unconscious* in the last few weeks with the result that there is hardly a WC in the house which is not 'hors de combat'.

Friday, 18th

Very bad raids on London for two nights now – they have hit St Paul's. I rang up my mother to see if she was all right and she sounded awfully tired. Lots of casualties at her First Aid Post. Thank goodness she's got Sidonie there to look after her, even if she does have to sleep on a camp-bed in the bathroom.

Saturday, 19th

A breakthrough! And it was me that did it, not Gussy!

It was my day off and I'd gone to spend a quiet afternoon browsing in the library for something not too heavy to read on night duty. Suddenly I spotted a familiar, lanky figure poring over Agatha Christie in one corner. As soon as he saw me he quickly disowned Poirot, and wandered off to join me by the travel section. My scalp tingled. A long elegant hand reached over my shoulder and pulled out a book. 'You should try this,' he said, 'it's frightfully good.' I took one look at the title – *The Gentle Savage* – and caught my breath.

'Yes, it is good, isn't it,' I said casually. 'My father wrote it.'

Massingham did a double take. 'You mean you're Dick Wyndham's daughter?' he exclaimed. Ah me, the old-boy network – it never fails!

'Yes,' I said, taking off my glasses and giving him that glazed myopic look which always makes people think that I'm a nymphomaniac.

It seems he has noticed me before. 'Don't you go round in a foursome? That clever-looking dark girl, what's her name, Bloch? And Moran – the one with the fair curls and the – er –'

'Yes, that's her,' I said.

'And the tall thin one – Lady Wynn-Waterlow's gel, isn't she?'

Snobbery is obviously Massingham's Achilles' heel. I felt the hook was now firmly in, especially when he mentioned casually that he would doubtless see me at the sergeants' dance.

Back to the billet I hared with the good news. Gussy was doing up her hair in pipe-cleaners, and Oscar was lying in bed with her glasses on the end of her nose, reading Rilke. Pandora was simply lying there looking cheesed-off, with bicycle clips on her pyjama bottoms to keep the fleas out.

'Guess who I just met in the library,' I panted, 'Massingham! And he thinks Bloch's brainy, Moran's sexy, and you and I are classy!'

Pandora shot up. 'God, that's wonderful, what a dark horse you are, Wyndham. Now all we've got to do is persuade him we're officer material.'

'Well, he'll be at the sergeants' dance, so we'll work on him there.'

As it happened, I very nearly didn't make it to the sergeants' dance at all.

I was skiving off housecleaning chores when Flight caught me, and I gave her such a dirty look that she put me on a 'fizzer' for dumb insolence. Pandora is even better at this than me. She just looks at them with her hands in her pockets and when they ask her name she spells it out very slowly as if she were giving it to a shop girl in Harrods. As her name is double-barrelled this drives them berserk.

Anyhow, there I was on the fizzer. The procedure is roughly as follows: the NCO to whom you have been insolent reports you, and you are then led before the Duty Officer, minus your hat, in case you throw it at her. (This is quite true, an officer once got a black eye through disregarding this precaution!) Then the sergeant who has put you on the fizzer tells her story which is listened to with rapt attention. You then tell a quite different story which nobody takes any notice of because they know it isn't true. You're then sentenced to – say – seven days' jankers, cleaning windows or peeling spuds and you are said to have 'had it'. This phrase can mean almost any form of misfortune – it is probably the most commonly used expression in the Air Force. Anyway, Flight told me I was lucky to get off with only two days, and not to miss the sergeants' dance.

Saturday, 26th

A lovely day, starting with chocolates and cigarettes in bed. Then we went out and picked the first violets for our buttonholes and spent the rest of the afternoon tarting ourselves up for the dance.

We had one lipstick between us – a Yardley's Cherry – with which to incarnadine our lips and cheeks. My hair was up in pipe-cleaners all day. I brushed it out at about six o'clock and poured Rubenstein's Apple Blossom all over it.

There is not much you can do to make a WAAF's uniform look sexy (apart from pulling your belt in till you can hardly breathe), but jumping up and down on your cap to loosen up the brim does help to give it a rakish air.

The sergeants' Mess Hall was hung with balloons and streamers left over from Christmas and a rather ropy band was playing on the platform. As we strolled in to the strains of Deep Purple it seemed that all the men were about five feet tall. Soon we were whirling around the room clasped to the amorous bosoms of these pint-size Romeos, dreaming all the time of our ideal, a mythical character whom we have christened Squadron Leader the Hon. Anthony Ashley-Dukes. Any minute now, we felt, he would swan in, so weighted with 'gongs' that he could hardly stand up, and sweep us off our feet. Meanwhile we have to put up with the sweaty embraces of these 'wingless wonders'. The very worst thing about being at a Filter Command is that there are no pilots! I can't describe the effect wings have on a WAAF. Our theme song should really be 'If I Only Had Wings'.

I was swept on to the floor by a tiny sergeant who – to my dismay – wanted to jitterbug. Soon we were surrounded by a circle of his mates, cheering him on with 'Get her, Peter boy!' and 'That's a nice bit of cuddle you've got tonight!'

It was at this unfortunate moment that the door swung open

and in came the next best thing to the Hon. Ashley-Dukes –
Massingham. He was with another girl and my heart sank. It took
three interminable dances, with me throwing meaningful looks
over the dwarf's shoulder, before I felt a hand on my arm and
there he was in all his glory asking me for a samba.

Later on when we were helping ourselves to burnt sausages at
the buffet, he asked me if I liked it at Preston.

'No, I hate it,' I said. 'We all hate it,' I added loyally.

'Well,' said the vision, 'have you ever thought of applying for a
commission? You know they're always on the lookout for keen
types.'

I could hardly contain my excitement as I told him how very
keen we were and how very much we would like to be officers
and right away he says he'll put in a good word for us. Even
better, he is going to let us do the serving at the next officers'
cocktail party and will introduce us to the 'right people'. Pandora,
Gussy and Oscar are over the moon.

Thursday, 1st May

The officers' cocktail party, a very pukka do indeed, with tents in
the garden in spite of the fact that it's still freezing cold. There was
lashings of punch, and things on sticks, and canapés, and bags of
gorgeous creatures with wings and medals and nicotine-stained
fingers stalking the lawn.

Our job was to serve drinks and hand round the canapés, but
it's really no fun at all watching your betters getting drunk and
wolfing down the caviar. Towards the end of the party we were
spending most of our time in the pantry, good and tight on the
dregs of the champagne cup, and ended up prostrate on the grass
behind the marquee, our pockets stuffed with sausages and cheese-
straws.

We were trying to say 'The Leith police dismisseth us' – without
much success – when who should stroll up but Massingham, asking
if we would like to be introduced to the CO! Great emptying of
pockets, tidying of hair and adjusting of kirbigrips, and off we

staggered to impress his nibs. He seemed a genial old soul – luckily half-cut himself – so I think we did all right. Now we can only wait and pray.

Saturday, 10th

Bags of panic! We were on watch when we heard that Hess had flown over from Germany.

Our CO, lean and aquiline, is a good pacer – he paced like mad, baring his teeth in fiendish glee and muttering, 'lengths of rubber tubing, by gad!' The girl who plotted Hess was thrilled to bits.

The same night they had a huge raid on London and got the Houses of Parliament and the Abbey – but *we* got thirty-three German planes. I rang up Mummy and thank God she was all right.

Tuesday, 27th

Huge excitement – we've sunk the *Bismarck*! Flight actually joined us in the pub and ordered drinks all round.

Tuesday, 3rd June

Just come off night watch, dog-tired. No sleep at all as there was a big raid on Manchester. Luckily my plotting is getting faster and more accurate, and I'm actually beginning to enjoy coping in a flap. We're working three days on, then a day off, then three nights, but even on our days off the bastards clobber us for PT and kit inspection.

As for our personal lives, they are a desert – not a boyfriend in sight! Massingham still gives us the odd conspiratorial smile over the Filter Room balcony, but rumour has it that he has been seen escorting a redhead from Signals. Gussy got off with a Polish rear-gunner at the Tower Ballroom in Blackpool, but she soon got tired of necking on the beach, and he couldn't afford a hotel. Pandora, Oscar and I lead lives of unmitigated chastity, our biggest weekly thrill being art classes held in a nearby Nissen hut by a very nice officer – ex-artist – called McNab.

Friday, 20th

Heatwave. Now that the summer has really started we all feel a bit more cheerful. In between watches we lie out in our bathing-dresses on the scrubby patch of grass outside our hostel, and are getting beautifully brown. Occasionally we stagger across the road to Mrs Stokes's cake shop, where the apple pies have given way to delicious strawberry tarts.

Another bright spot has been a letter from darling Rupert – it seems he has beaten me to it!

Darling Joanee,

Well, I'm an officer now! Went to a very cad tailor and got a uniform so smart and dashing you would swoon with desire to see me. I am very tough and cheery on my daily grog ration. I can climb masts, and toss kegs of butter around with one hand like Popeye. Actually, I am more or less in command of the boat as the Captain is always ashore poking. My mates call me 'The Dook', and win vast sums off me at an obscure game called 'Chase the Ace'. I don't do a lot of work. Most of the time I sit alone in my cabin with a bottle of whisky and a shot glass, playing the 'Study in Tremolo' on my guitar, while the crew murmur in the fo'c'sle. Write soon and tell me all about your glamorous social life in the WAAF.

Love
Rooples

Alas, our social life is not exactly whizz-o, though sometimes we hitchhike into Blackpool for the Tower Ballroom. On our last hitch we were standing on sacks of flour in an open lorry in the pouring rain, which didn't add to our glamour on the dance floor. (Oscar tried to hitch a funeral the other day – most unfortunate.)

Apart from that the highspots of our social life are pub parties given by the girls in our Mess, which usually turn out to be Babylonian orgies. Pandora, Oscar and I are not very good at these affairs where everybody kisses everybody else, no matter how repulsive. We eat and drink our way steadily through the 1/6d. worth we put into the kitty and look neither to right nor left. Gussy is a much better mixer, and she can also play the piano – 'Love's Old Sweet Song' on piano keys awash with beer. After the party the scene at the bus stop usually beggars description, WAAFs collapsing and being sick in the road, airmen peeing against the wall, couples rolling in the grass. Last time Pandora was sick all night from the pork pies.

Next morning we woke up at crack of dawn with the most appalling hangovers, and Pan was sick again in the transport taking us on watch. I took four aspirin but still had a raging headache – the table was crowded with Coastal Command aircraft on a training exercise. Blue, green, red and orange counters swam before my eyes, and I got told off by one of the nobs in the gallery for not getting them down fast enough.

We were recovering over strong tea in the canteen when Pandora rushed in and said she had just bumped into Massingham, who had told her that some new commissions would be coming through in a couple of months' time. We live in hope again!

Sunday, 22nd

Germany has invaded Russia! Churchill spoke to us on the wireless tonight saying we would give them full support.

Monday, 14th July

A wonderful parcel of goodies arrived from Mum recently, so I hastened to thank her.

Dearest Mummy,

Thanks for the lovely food parcel. We are still digging into the strawberry jam. We eat it at our midnight feasts with brown bread and butter and sardines, washed down with mugs of Symington's soup. We heat this up in the boiler room on piles of red-hot coals which we rake out on to the floor!

Well, unless I get a commission it looks as if I'm stuck in this hell-hole for good. What a shame you are so healthy or I could get a compassionate posting. Rhoda's mother has gallstones which is so useful for her. Couldn't you bribe a doc for a certificate? TB or something?!

Try and get me some more Sirdar wool (purple) for my jumper. I'm sure you could get it without coupons from Peter Jones if you buttered them up!

Thank goodness the raids on London seem to have petered out – I'm so relieved for you.

Lots of love to you and Sid, see you soon on leave,

Joan

PS. Just remembered a few more things! A subscription to *Horizon*, some sandwich spread, and any heavy rich fruit cake in large slabs!

Monday, 28th

A panicky phone call from Mummy. After weeks without any bombs they have just had a really bad raid, and she thinks I should postpone my leave – what a bind! She doesn't realise I'm not worried about the bombs, I'd just like to see her.

Monday, 22nd September

Still no news about our commissions. Everyone here is a bit depressed, especially with the Germans forging ahead in Russia. They took Kiev a few days ago, but found it had been left in ruins by the Russians. Flight, who fancies himself as a student of history, says the buggers had better watch out as it's beginning to snow there and look what happened to Napoleon.

Wednesday, 1st October

Any moment now I shall be twenty! I've written my mother a long letter, telling her exactly what I want – Hemingway's *For Whom the Bell Tolls*, or Graham Greene's *Brighton Rock*, any edition of Verlaine's poems (try Zwemmers), a record of Dinah Shore singing 'Yes My Darling Daughter' or Bing Crosby's 'Tumbling Tumbleweed'. Hope she gets the message! Luckily that raid on the 27th seems to have been the only one, so hope to see her and Sid soon, if this commission thing doesn't come up first.

Sunday, 2nd November

Today I saw my first dead body. A man was run over outside our hostel. I was walking along thinking about cakes for tea when I saw a motor-bike lying buckled on its side, and a man lying on a yellow satin cushion with the top of his head knocked off. The blood around him wasn't yet dry and someone had tried to cover it with sand. How weird that I should have gone through the Blitz without ever seeing anyone dead.

Massingham has been dropping heavy hints that new commission lists are expected soon, so we're keeping our fingers crossed.

Saturday, 15th

We've done it! Fourteen of us including Pandora, Oscar and me – but not poor Gussy – are to go up for commissions.

We were told to report to Flight Sergeant's office, and within hours we were in front of a Filter Commission Board in the CO's office – Squadron Leader Cholmondley and a few scientific observers. They fired technical teasers at us, gave us some tracks to filter, and then asked questions which were mostly snob-orientated. Only six of us were picked, our lot amongst them. Poor Gussy feels terrible but they've assured her she'll be on the list next time.

In three weeks it's Stanmore for our final Board. According to Flight, this one will be no picnic. A few very crooked gentlemen will be out to panic us. One, says Flight, called Squadron Leader Rudd, is the biggest bugger he's ever met, and the chief scientific observer is the cleverest man in England. He says – and I hope he's joking – that they fire off pistols behind your back to test your nerve.

Monday, 8th December

The Japs have dropped bombs on Pearl Harbor, and now the Yanks are finally in the war! What a relief not to be on our own any more. We declared war on the Japs at midnight.

Tuesday, 9th December

Our last night before the Board. I've had all my hair cut off, like a boy, and starched my collar extra stiff to impress the judges. Oscar says I look like a perverted choirboy.

We wanted to celebrate so we decided on a gay night out in Preston (the alternative being a dance at the local lunatic asylum). We started with tripe and onions at the Plaza, absolutely divine, with loads of chips. Then to the music hall to see something called Gaités de Montmartre. We had scenes of Apache life, a Burmese belly-dancer, and Famous Love Scenes through the ages, not to mention a final can-can. There was also a conjuror and a 'Mr Memory'. You sit in red plush seats and there are little numbers at the side of the stage saying what act is on, rather like the hymn board in church.

Gussy knew the conjuror so we went backstage and he took us to a pub next door, with six of the chorus girls in all their make-up, v. jolly. They had the most marvellous hot meat pies near the bus stop – soft, shiny pastry, and dark brown gravy that positively burst out of the top. We had just enough time to wolf them down before the bus came. Altogether a very good evening.

Wednesday, 10th

The great day has finally dawned. Oscar, Pan and I are off to Stanmore. We've been up all night studying wavelengths and frequencies by the light of a torch, as we are billeted in a convent with no light bulbs. All around us are the other candidates, bags of corporals and not an aircraftwoman in sight. We are the only 'plonks' and we are hoping the others here are as dumb as they look.

Up at 7 a.m. to get to Fighter Command by nine. Pandora, who has nervous diarrhoea (unlike me, who has nervous consti-pation), went hurrying off to the lavatory. Minutes later we heard anguished shrieks. Someone had left the window open and the seat was two feet under snow, with icicles hanging from the chain. Pan sat on it in the dark and her bum got frozen to the seat, which nearly made us late for the interview.

Off we set to walk to HQ through country lanes completely snowed-up and uphill all the way, lugging our heavy suitcases. Of course, I slipped and fell head first into a snowdrift, ruining my soignée appearance. After a mile of utter hell we reached Bentley Priory – a colossally imposing pile surrounded by armed cordons and barriers.

The dreaded Board took place in a room straight out of the Palace of Versailles, huge gilt mirrors, tapestries, miles of parquet.

And there right at the end, a tiny table with three sinister figures seated behind it. I walked the entire length under their concerted glares, petrified of slipping on the parquet in my snowy boots. As soon as I sat down they started firing questions at me, designed to test my intelligence and powers of observation.

'What is Pythagoras' theorem? Which end of a cow gets up first?' and so on.

Then comes technical stuff. Then snob stuff (school, father's occupation, etc.) and finally a written psychology paper. I kept telling them I was hopeless at arithmetic but they obviously thought I looked 'the type' and seemed reasonably impressed.

Sixteen hours later we were back in Preston, after a ghastly journey, to find frozen pipes, no working lavatories, and had to go straight on duty unwashed and without any sleep.

Saturday, 13th

We have passed, all three of us! Pretty good show, by gad! Flight is hysterical with pride – it is a great boost for Nine Group and he has promised to take us all out on an almighty drunken binge in Blackpool before we finally leave, which will be in about three weeks' time, just after Christmas.

Saturday, 3rd January 1942

Our last night. Flight remembered his promise, and took us all into Blackpool for a big celebration. A slap-up meal, a fortune-teller, and then had awful photos taken for sixpence on the front. After that the Tower Ballroom, where I danced for hours under the whirling lights with Welsh flight mechanics, Polish gunners, New Zealand pilots, and even Flight himself – a heady moment. Afterwards he took us to a little club he knew, where, as he had promised, he got us reeling, roaring drunk on rum and coke.

Now there is just one more hurdle, an Air Ministry Board to

see whether you are really a lady. They look out for dirty nails, holes in stockings and try to find out if your mother was a char, and ask you trick questions to see if you say 'toilet' or 'pardon'.

Then comes an intensive training course in Filter Room procedure, which we hear is pretty tough. Instead of putting down plots on the map we will be using arrows to show the exact position and course of each aircraft, and identifying them with a plaque.

After that it's admin stuff, boring things like taking parades, telling off WAAFs with dirty collars or too-long hair, kit inspection, and asking them if they've any complaints about the food. Needless to say, they have, but are usually too scared to say so. Luckily, once we are posted, we won't be expected to do an awful lot of that sort of thing, because we are what's rather grandly known as 'Special Duties'.

Wednesday, 18th March

Typically I got mumps halfway through my last week of training. I'd been feeling feverish for days, but put it down to the excitement. Then my face swelled up like a balloon and I was hauled off to the isolation hospital. Sister was a dragon, she came charging down the ward, doing a running commentary – you could hear her coming from afar. 'Good morning, Lieutenant, had your bowels open? Don't pick your nails, Eileen. What's this I hear about your refusing the bedpan, Wyndham?'

Finally the great day arrived, our training was over, and we were all set for the thin blue band, not to mention £2 14s. 10d. a week – though I understand that most of this goes on what's known as 'living up to your uniform'. Can't wait to live it up – let's hope I get posted near London.

BOOK II

April 1942

BENTLEY PRIORY, STANMORE

Well, here I am, an officer, and life is absolutely the cat's whiskers. I've been posted to Stanmore, near London, the top Fighter Headquarters in England. Bentley Priory is quite an awe-inspiring place, the whole Battle of Britain was masterminded from here. The Mess is a rambling old manor house, thatched and gabled with carved oak doors and twisted chimneys, the walls covered in wistaria. There are chestnuts on the lawn, and a stone terrace where we sip our drinks of an evening.

I nearly died of shock when I first walked into the Mess – all chintz sofas and blazing log fires – and a suave blonde walked up to me and said, 'Hello, Wyndham, how about a gin and lime?' The food is wonderful and booze flows in abundance. Our private sitting room is called the ante-room, large and sunny with a piano and a radiogram.

All my fellow officers are fairly glamorous and a gay, wild lot, always talking about the Savoy or the Berkeley, and the nightclubs they've been to. They are mad about swing and play hot jazz all day.

The Wrens, who share our Mess, are sniffy and stuffy, reading good books in one corner of the ante-room while the WAAFs go trucking madly around the gramophone singing 'Bounce Me Brother with a Solid Four'.

We have early morning tea in bed, and eggs, cornflakes, toast and marmalade for breakfast. All this and 7s. 10d. a day! I feel I am living in some wonderful dream.

At the moment I am in a temporary billet with Lady Welch, our senior WAAF officer, and as she's away I'm in her huge nuptial bed. I lie there gazing at her heavily gold-braided greatcoat hanging on the bedroom door and Lord W's hunting boots, but I expect I'll be moving into the Priory soon.

June 1942

Two months have passed and the gilt has slightly worn off the gingerbread. In the first place I miss Oscar and Pan terribly. They were posted to Inverness. The other girls here are reasonably friendly, but terribly posh and debby – not really my style. My room-mate, Tessa, is a good type, but very 'county' and talks a lot about horses and hunting. I can see she thinks I am a bit strange because I read Baudelaire in bed. Apart from squabbles over who'll have the basin first for washing out bras and knickers we don't communicate much. I haven't palled up with anyone else, and what's more, I don't even have a boyfriend!

Lately there has been yet another influx of new blood, great strapping girls who arrive with their own horses and dogs and sit in the Mess of an evening playing poker, drinking double whiskies and doing all but crack a stock-whip to summon the orderly.

As for the work, it is much more hectic than in Preston, with sweeps over France every day and our bombers going out every night. It's terribly hot in the underground Filter Room and I'm not wearing anything under my uniform except thin pants and a suspender belt, but still my shirt comes off wringing wet. It's awful, but thank goodness we are allowed to work in our shirt-sleeves. I sometimes wonder if I am up to the work. When I come off the table, my hands are shaking like crazy.

To make matters worse, one of the officers has got it in for me. Her name is Barbara Stead, known as the Bedstead. She is very large with a slight moustache, and she seems to think I am a 'bad type'. I sometimes catch her watching me in a funny sort of way, and as she is considerably senior, this makes me very nervous. So there it is, after all my high hopes I find myself guilt-ridden, lonely and bored stiff. Something has got to happen soon to make life more exciting again.

Thursday, 9th July

Schoenberg's 'Pierrot Lunaire' was the start of it all. Starved of culture I suddenly decided to go up to London and attend the most incomprehensible and esoteric concert I could find. 'Pierrot Lunaire' seemed to fit the bill, as apparently it has neither tune, shape nor harmony.

The Aeolian Hall was sold out, and I waited an hour for returns without success. Wandering disconsolately down Bond Street, I turned to look into a shop window and saw the reflection of a little, ugly man. Apparently he also saw mine and suffered a 'coup de foudre'. As he had also been unable to get a ticket he was not at a loss for an opening gambit.

Five minutes later we were walking down Bond Street together, an incongruous pair, and I was wondering how to shake him off.

Ten minutes later I was saying to myself, 'Hell! I've been respectable for far too long, it's about time I reverted to type.' Need I say that this chap was wearing green corduroy trousers, a red tie and a beret and hadn't had a haircut for weeks? Of course not. It was just like the good old days in Redcliffe Road, when I went around with 'bad types' like Rupert and Gerhardt.

Fifteen minutes later we were approaching Soho and the little man was saying, 'What about a stroll through these sleazy streets, redolent of Balzac and his prostitutes, and a bite to eat at that famous and extremely cheap haunt of the intelligentsia, the Shanghai Chinese Restaurant?' I said it suited me fine and soon found myself sitting in my spotless officer's uniform between a huge negro in a bowler hat and my little man, who was now feverishly writing poetry on pieces of orange paper. The restaurant and the tablecloths were filthy, the food delicious — seaweed soup and tea with flowers in it.

Over the soup he suddenly said, 'Would you mind if I asked you to look at me, or have you been taught it is more ladylike to keep the face averted?' Actually I was busy eating but stopped to take off my glasses and give him a quick myopic flash. 'Ah,' he groaned, 'your eyes are so deep that when I throw a glance into them I cannot hear it hit the bottom.'

It appears he is a Yugoslav and his name is Petya. He is about four and a half feet high, a dwarf really, and just turned twenty. He is ugly as – well no, not really – his eyes are beautiful and he has nice hair. Needless to say, he is an artist, and he thinks that one of the pictures in his studio will start a whole new era in art!

After lunch he took me to Regent's Park and we walked round and round the ornamental duckpond telling each other the story of our lives. He said he finally 'found' himself after sitting for three weeks under an umbrella tree reading Jung's *Science of Life*, and playing the Beethoven C minor quartet.

When he was fifteen his father gave him a huge studio with a ceiling of beaten silver and black velvet walls, but he still wasn't happy because none of the girls at college would dance with him as he was so small. 'So what did you do?' I asked. 'I decided to be a genius,' he replied. 'But first I slept with all the tallest prostitutes in Venice.'

By six o'clock we were walking round and round Baker Street Underground Station talking about frigidity in women. Just before the train came in he cried, 'Look at that young green sapling growing by the railway track, lured upwards by a melancholy and hopeless tropism, a desire of the moth for the candle, the sunflower for the sun, man for woman! I might even dare to say that the lime-green shoots of renewed hope are beginning to show their heads again above the dark abysses of my soul. Well, here comes the train, I suppose you couldn't lend me a pound, could you?'

I walked back to Stanmore laughing to myself a lot, but in a state of curious elation.

When I got to the Priory I found a gramophone concert going on in the baronial hall, a log fire blazing, and records of *La Bohème*, Tchaikovsky and *Les Sylphides* – like ghosts of a lost world. Memories of sitting in the gallery at Covent Garden with my mother, bewitched by Massine and Markova.

After all these months of 'waafing' I found the music difficult to catch on to, just as people who have been ill for a long time find it difficult to do the things they used to be good at. I'd forgotten anything I ever knew about form, harmony and all the rest. Just pure sensuous enjoyment is all I have at the moment. Perhaps Petya will help me to get back in touch with myself again.

Saturday, 11th

He rang, and wants me to go to his studio, somewhere in north London. I'll try and wangle a day pass.

Saturday, 18th

It was a shock when Petya opened the door. I'd forgotten how tiny he was, like a little boy. The mirrors in his room were so low I had to stoop to arrange my hair. It is a very small studio, at the top of the house, full of skulls and death-masks and some of his own very peculiar paintings.

The one which he sets such store by (which will set the world on fire) is magnificent technically, but I found the contents rather shocking. 'It reminds me of sheep's kidneys,' I said rather tactlessly. He handed me a magnifying glass. 'Look closely, it's the same technique as Titian used,' he said, but I really couldn't make head or tail of it.

After that we had lunch, which was baked beans on toast, and then, because the studio was freezing, he wrapped me in a blanket and made me lie on the bed while he played me the Dvořák violin concerto, staring into my face all the time. He had taken his glasses off and looked quite different, almost attractive. I could feel the current from his body, so hot it almost set my teeth aching.

'Oh, I'm so happy,' he finally said. 'It's so wonderful for us to be together, quite naturally like this, without my seeing in your eyes that look that all other women seem to get which means that they crave immediate sexual intercourse.'

I felt very relieved to hear that.

'You are so amazingly alive,' he went on. 'You don't have that mask that most people walk around with that takes six whiskies to dissolve. You haven't the slightest idea who you are, so I will have to make you many mirrors.'

I was beginning to feel very tired and wished he would stop, but now he was stroking my forehead and saying, 'Oh you miracle, you just don't know how to frown, do you?'

Leaning forward he kissed me lightly and quickly. 'Do I get my face slapped?' Surprisingly I didn't flinch away. Of all the things that might have happened this is the strangest, that I should like – and even feel physically attracted to – a little ugly man. I'd always held physical beauty to be the one essential. But here was Petya kissing me and his kisses were not repulsive.

Hours later he looked up and said, 'Do you think you could ever love me? What does it depend on?'

I told him rather tactlessly that I'd always loved people for their good looks and pleasant company.

'Not much hope for me,' he murmured bitterly. 'Though I am, of course, of excellent family, and possibly a genius.'

Just then the door opened and a whey-faced woman with straight greyish hair and what appeared to be one eye put her face around the door, saw I was there, and went out again, shutting the door with unnecessary vigour.

'Who's that?' I asked.

'Oh,' said Petya nervously, 'that's my landlady, Ethel. I have told her you are a lady from the cultural section of the Ministry of Information. Would you mind if we went out and sat by the canal for a bit? She's terribly jealous of me.'

After an hour of sitting by the canal listening to Petya talking about art, while being eaten alive by mosquitoes, I told him I was ravenous, so we went to the Ceylon café in Camden Town – a hole in the wall, where negroes in beautiful grey suits talked to handsome half-caste seamen.

In the underground he kissed me till the last train went, sitting in the dark – he had to sit to be able to reach me. The train came

26

in with a warm rush of wind, and in its light his face was dream-like, a changeling.

I went straight on to night duty – the Filter Room was in a state of furious activity. Five planes had been shot down, maybe more, I moved quickly to my position and began to sort out the tracks. The plaques and arrows swam before my eyes, and my mind kept drifting back to Petya. Came off at five and slept like the dead until midday.

Saturday, 25th

Petya and I saw *This Gun for Hire* at the Forum cinema. Afterwards we strolled down the Fulham Road and as we were passing the Servite church a terrific storm broke, with pink lightning forking over the roof tops and hailstones rattling down.

We rushed into the church for shelter, and I told Petya how this was where I was baptised. 'I'll drain the font dry,' he cried, as the lightning flashed behind the stained glass windows. Then he lit a candle for Soeur Thérèse because she was so pretty, and I kissed St Peter's toe, and Petya tried to drag me into the confessional and kiss me while the lay brother wasn't looking.

The storm was abating. We went down the road to Finch's pub where he made me very drunk on double whiskies – it must have been about then that I suddenly decided I would like to sleep with him. He had been telling me how frightened he was because he was ugly and two feet too small and sooner or later he would get on my nerves. I suddenly felt how nice it would be to give him a treat.

We rolled drunkenly back to the studio, clutching an enormous can of beer. Petya put a pink scarf over the lamp and I tuned the radiogram to a jazz programme.

Whilst I was slipping out of my clothes he kept saying, 'Don't if you don't want to. Please don't. It's still not too late.' But I went ahead anyway and soon we were both naked. Petya looks much better without his clothes, he is strong and muscular, with a smooth chest and very narrow flanks. His lovemaking was very athletic, and, I'm sure, technically wonderful, but sadly wasted on me! In spite of all the weird and strange positions I remained as frigid as ever, which surprised him considerably. He kept apologising, thinking it was his fault, until I explained that I had never had an orgasm. 'We'll soon fix that,' he promised, opening the can of beer and switching on the Beethoven C minor quartet. He wanted to drink beer from between my breasts but instead we drank it from the cat's bowl. Then we danced mad Cossack dances, still naked, and he arched my body and stood me on my head and made love to me again. Very exhausting, very uncomfortable and I still didn't have an orgasm.

I felt so sorry and so guilty about this, after all his trouble, but when he said, 'Darling, I do love you so frightfully,' I managed to say 'I love you too,' although it wasn't true. The blood rushed to his head and he said, 'God, it must be the Beethoven!'

He thinks my frigidity was all brought on by my convent education, but nothing that couldn't be helped by psychoanalysis and lots of straightforward intercourse. 'Progressive poking', as dear old Rupert would have said. Personally, I think it's a lot of nonsense and Petya will wear himself to a shadow unnecessarily, but he assures me that with my good body and courageous soul I am made for love. If only they can be co-ordinated I will be a masterpiece. I know, of course, that it's all hooey but I would like to have an orgasm before I die.

Oh yes, I've got to write down all my dreams, which will be difficult as I don't seem to be getting much sleep.

The thunder broke again as I got back to the Mess. Had to sit through an RAF lecture on the heights of aircraft (a difficult thing for an officer to estimate), which was like a nightmare. I kept going to sleep and waking up again, dreaming of love and art and music, then awaking to cut-off angles and alphas and BDFs. Sometimes I hate and fear the work and the people here. I have not slept for two and a half days and I've noticed the Bedstead giving me some very strange looks.

Monday, 27th

To make matters worse, I was summoned yesterday to the Codes and Ciphers Office, where a fiercely suspicious Flight Sergeant was brandishing a telegram from Petya. It was, they feared, some mysterious code. He read it out to me, letter by letter. 'Nulla potest mulier tantum se dicere amatum.' This didn't sound quite right to me, but I got the gist, and explained that it's by Catullus and means no one has ever loved a woman as much as my boyfriend loves me.

Flight looked sour and said, 'Tell 'im to use the King's English next time!'

It was beautifully hot so I sunbathed in my bathing dress on Petya's lawn – Ethel glaring down from the top window. Petya brings me flowers he has pinched from the next-door garden. We drink Ovaltine and watch ants. Petya thinks I am beautiful in my bathing dress because I am so nice and brown.

After a while he asks me about my dreams. 'It's very difficult,' I said, 'as soon as I wake they start vanishing back into my subconscious, and it's very rarely I can catch one by the heels before it disappears.' However, I remember that last night I was piloting a plane which went into a spin and started to fall. Then suddenly the joy-stick, which was very large, came alive in my hand, full of power and vigour, and I landed the plane safely. Petya seems awfully chuffed about the joy-stick and said it was most significant.

I would like to have slept in the garden all day, but after the usual lunch of baked beans he insisted on making love to me.

It was very cold and clinical, and he experimented on me as if I were an amoeba under a microscope. He would interrupt intercourse deliberately while checking on my pulse-beat, on the principle that a disappointment will make you want something twice as much, and was delighted to notice a certain quickening. He also asked me to describe in clinical detail all my previous affairs and what I had felt. As I had only had one it didn't take long.

By now I was almost dropping from lack of sleep, and was finding his questions rather humiliating. In revenge I told him how I loathed analytical people and questions without answers. He winced as if I had struck him.

'I must apologise,' he whispered, 'I've been causing you a lot of pain and what is worse, boredom, especially as I and my life are nothing but a question without an answer.'

What a bitch I am! I'm not in love with him yet I'm letting him rearrange his whole life around me. I would like to be able to love him because he's one of the decentest people I ever came across, and though this may sound extravagant, I think he is perhaps a genius.

Later he stood me dinner at the Czardas, pork goulash and dumplings. It seems he comes here often with his Hungarian friend Zoltan. Apart from me, Zoltan seems to be the greatest thing in Petya's life. He is so brilliant, so handsome, such a loyal friend. Apparently he has told Zoltan all about me, and he can't wait for us to meet.

Tessa is fascinated by my descriptions of Petya. He and his kind are quite outside her experience. She also says I'm looking awful, and ought to get more sleep – love and work just don't mix, she tells me. I realise this only too well, as my trembling fingers reach for another arrow, and the multi-coloured plots blur before my eyes. Sometimes when the 'gods' in the gallery think you really can't cope they send down someone to help you out, and this has been happening to me far too often lately.

Thursday, 30th

My week's leave is coming up soon, thank God, but I have rashly promised to spend it with Petya. He says we've got to take a room because of Ethel. Is Ethel his mistress? I ask myself. We wandered through Chelsea eating cherries and looking for digs, and finally ended up in Oakley Street at a brothel owned by old Mabel Lethbridge, whose telegraphic address used to be 'CHASTITY, LONDON'. I didn't know if it was still a brothel, so I pretended to be Petya's wife, and we booked a lovely room with a window looking on to the garden, a patchwork quilt, a wireless, and a copy of Kipling's *If* over the bed. Dylan Thomas lives here too but I think he's away at the moment.

I was supposed to meet my father for lunch at the Café Royal but when I got there I was met by Peter Quennell, tall and soigné in black, who told me that Daddy had had a relapse and would I go round to the London Clinic instead. He has had a nervous breakdown and been invalided out of the army.

He was lying in bed wearing his major's tunic over his pyjamas, his hair white and his face very brown, looking extremely distinguished but with bad teeth. He was a bit doped up and couldn't talk much but we've arranged to meet during my leave, when they let him out.

Saturday, 1st August

Leave started, and I arrived with my bags at Oakley Street. Felt strange and self-conscious at being alone with Petya in this lovely room which was to be our home for the next week. He sat by the window, I sat at his feet looking up at a drawing of the 'Kerry Lute Player'. I felt lost and gloomy. We quarrelled — I had an awful feeling that I had made a foolish mistake and should never have come.

. The trouble was that I had visited Annie (Rupert's new girl-friend) in her studio that morning, and among a litter of bottles from last week's party I had heard all the gossip, news of Rupert and the old gang, and it had given me terrible nostalgia for the good old days. Annie has a Hindu poet called Subra living with her, very filthy — and Rupert is in Scotland in a military hospital — he will soon be invalided out. I am longing to see him again. Meantime I felt full of vague misery but not quite sure what was the matter with me.

Petya has asked Zoltan to come tomorrow, so I shall meet him at last. I'll probably be disappointed in him — he has been represented to me as something so very special and fascinating. I asked Petya what he looked like and he said, 'Like Cesare Borgia, always very well dressed, quiet and soigné, with a dark beard.'

In the evening I put on my grey crêpe dress with daisies on it and a coral necklace, and met my father at the Café Royal. Over pink gins we talked for the first time in our lives like friend to friend instead of father to child. It was so funny, so restful to find a person just like myself, with my own faults, and capable of understanding them – even though we hadn't met for years.

I told him all about Petya, and he made me promise that if I ever got into trouble, or was going to have a baby, I would come to him for help. He kept wondering what I would have been like if he had brought me up instead of my religious mother, and how sad it was that she was never able to marry again.

Then to the Swiss where we had whisky, and Dick – I really can't call him Daddy – was very amused to find out what an expensive drinker I am. He kept saying, 'Now be careful, Joanie! Remember it runs in the family! Take warning by poor old Nina Hamnett over there. You know it really puzzles me how you ever got into this milieu – I mean the Swiss pub, and so on – it's so far removed from your mother's world.'

I told him how I had escaped from all that and he laughed and said, 'You know, you're exactly like your Aunt Bunch.' That alarmed me a bit as everyone knows poor Bunch was partial to drink and negroes. Not negroes actually, my father said, negresses, and he told me about her running off to Harlem with a black actress, and living with her there.

Just then Annie and Subra breezed in looking particularly decadent and dirty. I waved to them and Dick said rather apprehensively, 'That's not your set, is it, Joanie?' I assured him they were only casual friends.

Dinner at Gennaro's, lobster and white wine. The head waiter gave me a carnation.

We finished up at the Gargoyle, going up in a little lift to a bar full of Matisse drawings. 'This is your cousin, David Tennant,' my father said, 'he owns the place.'

David shook my hand in a distracted way. 'Excuse me a minute, you see there's this girl I'm after, I think she's hiding somewhere.' Just then a distraught-looking blonde broke cover and raced for the stairs, my cousin halloo-ing after her.

By this time I was so drunk I was verging on insensibility. With great difficulty we navigated the glassy staircase that went down to the little dance floor. With amazing equilibrium I piloted my father around the floor, moving as if in a dream. Both of us were stinko paralytico. Alexander's Band played a rude song called 'If You Want It You've Got to Buy It', with a chorus that goes:

You can have it in a saucer
You can have it in a cup,
You can have it lying down
Or you can have it standing up.

When we got upstairs, Philip Toynbee was being sick on the sofa, so we left hurriedly.

I steered Dick through the Soho streets, his big feet splaying out left and right. Both of us very cheery and happy and ignoring the dope pedlar who called to us from the doorway of Ley-Ons. It seemed as if we had known each other all our lives. In the taxi I lay against his shoulder and he kissed my hair and forehead. Then, because he was so drunk, I suppose, he began to kiss me properly as if I were a girlfriend or something – it was terribly embarrassing. I think he was so drunk he didn't know who he was with. Then we got to Oakley Street and it looked so gloomy in the dark I dreaded going in.

'What do you do all day there?' Dick asked. Then he laughed. 'Make love, I suppose.' He kissed my forehead again and I stumbled out, fishing the key out of the letterbox on the end of a piece of string.

By now I was deadly sick. I managed to reach the bathroom where I immediately passed out on the floor and was unconscious for two hours. When Petya came home he undressed me and put me to bed where I talked incoherently. Then, he said, I put my arms around his neck and my head on his shoulder like a little woolly lamb and went straight to sleep, snoring loudly.

Sunday, 2nd

Woke next morning feeling bloody awful and stayed in bed till teatime with a wet flannel on my head. Then I got up to make myself look swell for Zoltan in my lace blouse and navy blue trousers.

I came down from the bathroom, clean and fresh and with apple-blossom scent on. I'd set my hair so that it was nice and curly and brushed up and Petya said, 'You're looking your best, darling.'

I was making toast by the fire when Zoltan came. He walked in quietly, took my hand and sat down, seeming to fold in on himself. I gave him some cocoa and he sat with his knees together, his arms close to his side, bent over the steaming mug and holding it between thin hands. He was completely different from the flamboyant person I had imagined. He was dark, with straight brown hair, soft and fine, flopping over his forehead, and a beard like a Russian Christ. Very pale with the most amazing grey eyes, large and shadowy, and long white hands. He must be quite a bit older than Petya, and unlike him, he is thin and fairly tall, and his clothes are good – everything about him clean and fastidious.

When he smiled you felt your heart melt within you, but at the same time it was a treacherous smile like some beautiful fawning dog. He has the attraction of the devil in his eyes and in his smile, and in his slow sleepy voice with its fascinating accent, but all the time I was aware of a soft, weak, dangerous streak in him. He kept watching me. I found it difficult to make conversation and every other minute our eyes met. I knew it would be like this from the first time Petya mentioned him to me.

He looked at my drawings and told me they were good. Petya had told me no man in England knows more about art and aesthetics, so I was pleased.

Went to the Nelson and sat at a corner table. Quentin Crisp was there with his hair down to his shoulders. Petya, who hardly ever drinks, became very wild and insulted people. But Zoltan, who can hold his drink and is nearly killing himself with it, merely became more calm and dignified than before and talked more amusingly, buying whisky after whisky and trying to make me do the same – but I was still suffering from a dreadful hangover.

A bit later he turns to me and says, 'I must tell you, you are very beautiful.'

'You see,' says Petya, 'I've not been lying to you.'

'Tell me, Petya, are you a very possessive chap?'

'What's the matter with you? Do you want to sleep with Joan?'

'Ah, sleep! You are a crude fellow. Besides, I'm your best friend. You remember the man who slept with a sword between him and his friend's wife?'

'Well, you can have any other of my girls but not Joan.'

Then Zoltan starts telling me how I must always stay with Petya. 'Believe me, Joan, this boy is silly and he is too young but he will be one of the greatest painters of the next twenty years.'

Then they embrace and Petya kisses my hand and we are all drunk and sentimental together.

When we left the pub it was late but the light lingered. We felt safe, for there have been no raids for ages, thank God. Zoltan took all the loose change out of his pockets and threw it laughingly into the bushes. Then he smiled into the fascinated face of a baby over its mother's shoulder and said, 'Goodnight my little one – it is night and yet it is still day. I hate this day. Come night, night, night! Of all the hours in my life this hour when the pubs close is the saddest.'

The baby blinked at him and he said, smiling, 'All your life you will remember this, if only in your dreams.' The baby started to howl, so Zoltan hastened on.

Back in our room there is a clock, its intricate gold wheels exposed under a glass dome, its hands stopped at midnight. Zoltan kisses it, murmuring, 'My dearest clock, you have died at midnight and so shall I! God I'm thirsty. I've got to have a drink. Petya, I'm thirsty, give me a word to end the day. . . .'

'Sous une lumière blafarde,' says Petya, his eyes fixed on the painted door under the glaring light, and just then it bursts open and a blonde bus conductress staggers in and says, 'Ooh, isn't this my room, where's Fiddler and what have you done with my iron?'

Zoltan held her by the leg and said, 'Sleep with me tonight, you gorgeous creature.' But she said, 'Not bloody likely,' and escaped after a brief struggle.

Then a whole crowd arrived next door for a party and started playing the gramophone very loudly, and Zoltan, putting his tragic face round the door, says, 'My child is sick, she will die, why are you so noisy?' In fact by now he is into a lot of stupid tricks, turning on the gas and pretending to inhale it while Petya throws up his hands in despair. And there is much talk as to whether he should stay and sleep on the floor, but we finally dispose of him and in the hall he looks at me with his sad eyes and kisses my hands, thanking me for the evening.

I was bemused and unhappy, so Petya, thinking to cheer me up, taught me how to make love according to an old Chinese book, in six simple stages. They didn't sound too simple to me, incredibly complicated in fact, and far too much like hard work. After it's all over, apparently, the woman must be very gentle and not kiss the chap passionately. I should hope not! A nice cup of tea would be far more welcome, I'd imagine.

Friday, 7th

Unhappily I now love Zoltan. I saw it coming; it was inevitable.

All morning I've wandered around in my dressing-gown, forlornly kissing the glass dome of the clock where he had kissed it, and seeing no solution to the problem. But it almost made me happy to have someone to love again, even if it is hopeless.

Petya seems to notice nothing. He came bouncing down from his bath to announce that we were going over to the studio for a seminar – lots of interesting young people discussing art – tea and cakes afterwards. The only snag was Ethel, who might prove tricky, but he didn't think she'd dare throw a scene in front of so many people.

Only one question burned on my lips: would Zoltan be there? But I dared not ask it. Still not knowing, I walked into the seminar with my eyes cast down, and only saw his shoes. They had to be his because they were clean and brightly polished and everybody else was in sandals.

Beautiful girls and ugly men were sitting all over the floor discussing the relationship between science and art. Petya leant back against my knees and talked about catharsis. Every now and then he would jump up and flash a slide on to a small screen – rats' foetuses, chicken embryos and so on.

A dapper little man was heckling him, and Petya kept muttering, 'Please, somebody watch out for that man, I didn't invite him and he is a well-known kleptomaniac.'

I was wearing my red corduroy trousers so as to blend in with the scene. I felt madly elated, arguing and talking my head off, most unlike my usual quiet self. Zoltan, who was leaning against the mantelpiece, never said a word but his eyes never left my face.

Suddenly there was the sound of a violent scuffle from the direction of the kitchen where Petya had gone to make the tea. I heard Ethel's voice screaming and Petya cursing in a foreign language, and then he came rushing out, holding his arm and looking quite white with rage.

'She took a breadknife to me,' I heard him mutter to Zoltan, 'and then she bit me! Can you get Joan out of here quickly, just for a few hours? You don't mind, do you? You can come back later when she's calmed down.'

Zoltan didn't look as if he minded at all, and before I could really take it all in he was steering me firmly down the stairs and into the street.

'What a strange situation! What would you like to do? A film, a meal, theatre? For myself, I feel like being utterly vulgar – all that arty stuff of Petya's gets on my nerves.'

To my amazement we headed for the West End, and Zoltan bought two of the cheapest seats for *No Orchids for Miss Blandish*.

'I had no idea you liked bad plays,' I said in amazement.

'But of course, my dear! There's nothing like a George Black show to take away the taste of Petya's little seminar. Would you like some chocolates?'

We sat in the gods and I enjoyed watching Zoltan the great aesthete smoking small black cigars and chuckling with delight as the lady in primrose satin scanties implored the villain not to fry her lover's face with an electric heater. I hoped Zoltan might hold my hand, but he acted throughout like a kindly uncle.

When we got back the students had all gone but Petya was still keyed up, wanting to talk about beauty, and symbols for the transformation of energy. Suddenly I thought, 'This boy is *silly, silly, silly*. I'll have to be careful or I'll lose my sense of humour.'

I'm still waiting and hoping for some sign from Zoltan, but nothing. He went home almost immediately, leaving me confused and distraught.

Saturday, 8th

A hot day and the three of us went to Kew. I'd woken up crying and felt unable to say a word. Zoltan was cold to me. I had a sudden revulsion against him. Perhaps I don't love him any more. An awful gloom came over me and I couldn't talk.

Meanwhile Petya and Zoltan were having metaphysical discussions and I was bored, bored. I wondered what would happen if I started talking about the Americans landing at Guadalcanal yesterday – but somehow I didn't think they'd be interested.

Suddenly Zoltan turned on me. 'Why do you never speak, or say anything exciting? Do you feel nothing, have you no emotions? I am really disappointed in you. I am going home, my friends.'

This nearly broke my heart, but Petya said something rapidly in Yugoslav and Zoltan sat back on the grass again. But for me the world had turned to ashes. Zoltan found me dull and unfeeling.

Zoltan was quoting *Samson Agonistes* – 'Oh, dark, dark, dark amidst the blaze of noon' – and I made the mistake of saying I thought Milton dull. 'Dull? You find this poem *dull*? It is a cold marble and a sharp mirror – it is so great that it nearly approaches silence.' After this I felt terribly crushed and didn't dare open my mouth again.

We went to the Orchid House but I was impervious to the beauty of leaves like giant tea trays, intricate orchids, lotuses as blue as light. I felt faint in the clammy heat.

The Chinese pagoda was surrounded by a fence topped with sharp spikes. Zoltan, his face Christ-like, laid the palm of his hand on one of the points and slyly looked up at me. His eyes smiled and invited, he nodded at me secretively. Without a word I laid my fist on the back of his hand and hammered it down on to the spike with great force. He cried out. Then, having looked at his palm, he gently fitted it back in exactly the same position, his eyes asking me to do it again. Then he walked away, smiling at me like a conspirator and rubbing his palm.

We went to the Swiss pub, and Petya was despatched to fetch the drinks. I sat and looked out of the window.

After a long silence Zoltan turned his seductive eyes on my face and murmured, 'Joan, will you please let me have your address? I want to write to you.'

I said yes, as in a dream, my heart beating madly. Suddenly every cloud had lifted.

'How much nicer Joan is when she is happy,' Petya observed coming back with the drinks.

'For me she is always nice,' Zoltan said. 'Such a pity her leave ends tomorrow.'

Midnight

Now I am alone with Petya. How can I bear it?

He leaves the wireless on so that the light from it will fall on my face. This is the strangest night I have ever spent. I loved Zoltan and it stared out from my eyes, sad and unmistakable. My mind was full of him, his every gesture and intonation, and the tears gathered at the corners of my eyes but did not fall.

Petya saw this and said, 'I can feel love coming from you tonight, Joan, it comes over me like a keen sweet wind. Tonight I've begun to feel that we really belong to each other.'

A shudder went through me and I tried to turn off the light, but he protested, saying that he must see my face.

'Tonight you're not of this earth – there has never been a night like this one. If only I could make it last forever.' And still I could not keep the love from my eyes that was for Zoltan, and the irony and the pity of it gave me an emotion that was almost painful in its intensity.

He wanted me to say something tender to him but I was speechless.

'Darling,' he kept saying, 'does this night mean nothing to you? These few moments are worth all the suffering in the world to me and I have suffered so little for them – but I will pay, like Faust, with my soul.'

And I thought, yes, I'm afraid you will. And feeling things that I hardly understood I lay over him and gave him thrill after thrill until he was panting and exhausted in my arms.

'You were marvellous, darling – really marvellous. What did you feel?'

'Nothing,' I said. 'I just like to give you pleasure.'

Petya yawned. 'That is a very masculine perversion,' he said, and so we went to sleep.

Wednesday, 12th

BENTLEY PRIORY, STANMORE

I told myself that Zoltan wouldn't write, and threw myself with fresh enthusiasm into the work routine. 'Now you're back from leave, Wyndham,' the Bedstead told me sternly, 'you'd better pull your socks up. Not been exactly pulling your weight lately, have you?'

So I pulled away like mad. Every day Hurricanes from Tangmere and Northolt were streaming over the Channel, and I worked well and furiously. Tuesday night was the busiest, with Beaufighters from Coastal Command torpedoing a German convoy – no sleep at all. Staggering to bed next morning I spotted a slim blue envelope sticking out of my cubby-hole. Zoltan's handwriting was neat and tiny.

My dear Joan, he wrote. . . .

It is a sad and beautiful night, moon very low and last train gone, so I walk very slowly thinking of you in that darkened room with Petya. I have so much to tell you but have I the right or the recklessness to do so? I feel like Actaeon when he comes upon Diana bathing.

What do you want of me, oh virginal goddess, are you bloodthirsty or tender? How everything that we two lived through during the last few days was dreamlike and painfully wild.

Night again, trees stand still, I think clean and calming thoughts of your eyes and your hands. Soon it will be day, little flowers drop dew and birds will soon awake. And I am the gentle breeze which comes from far, from very far, I am the gentle breeze which flies over forests and gardens, crossing brooks and lakes, entering houses, moving the curtains and touching gently the temples of those who are asleep.

I wait for your letter, dear Joan: write or telegraph and I will come to you.

Yours,
Zoltan

I found his letter strangely stilted, almost affected. It did not read like the Zoltan I thought I knew.

Nevertheless I am determined to see him, and will have to rearrange my watches accordingly. This will mean working eight hours today, five tonight, eight again tomorrow, with no sleep at all. It is a bit worrying because when I'm tired I get irritable and cope with the work rather badly, especially with the huge blitzes we are having in the south just now. Nevertheless, I wrote to Zoltan telling him to come on Saturday.

Saturday, 15th

It rained. I waited for him at the bus stop for what seemed hours, and then when I had given up hope I saw him come running, breathless with apologies. As we walked towards the Common he said, 'You are so beautiful it is almost too painful to look at you.'

41

He speaks quietly and with difficulty, so that one imagines he is sincere. But how can he be sincere when he pretends to be Petya's best friend? And now he is telling me that he has never even liked him!

'It is strange how Petya thinks I'm his best friend,' he says, as if reading my thoughts. 'I never have been.'

And I remember the night we met and Petya saying to me, 'Now you have met my only friend! How lucky I am with such a girl and such a friend.'

So it was all false and Zoltan is a liar and now he comes to me behind Petya's back to talk about chastity and beauty and the old, old gag about not spoiling a beautiful flower. What I have done is even worse, because I know I can't resist Zoltan and I knew from the start that I would leave Petya for the first good-looking man that came along.

And now Zoltan is off on a new tack: 'You are so clean and unspoilt. And because you are pure and untouched we all want to get our hands on you to spoil you and make you dirty. Isn't it so? But you must stay as you are always, always – you are such a dear child.'

Phooey! And damn him, I want him so badly. There is something in his smile that frightens me, a gentle cruelty. He says himself that he is a scoundrel but a kind one. That, I feel, is the worst sort. I am in a nice mess. I don't want to hurt Petya but my God I'm going to. I shall probably get hurt too but I don't care.

I led him through the woods to a little pub called The Case is Altered, and at a table with yellow roses he shot me a very good line over some very bad sherry. He even told me his wife didn't understand him! And how she'd tried to poison herself, and how he'd nearly died of stomach cancer. Then with obsessive venom he returned to the subject of Petya.

'How could you go with Petya when he is living with Ethel? Yes, of course he lives with her, in fact she probably keeps him. You must never force yourself to sleep with someone out of pity – it is terrible – promise me you will never do it again. And forget all this psychoanalysing nonsense. It's wrong and harmful. Things must come naturally and not be forced.

'How strange you were sitting by the fire in Oakley Street and saying nothing! It is unhealthy for you, a girl of twenty, to live with Petya. Did you realise that he told me every single physical detail of his affair with you?'

By now I hardly knew whom I disliked most, Petya or Zoltan. Zoltan is fine in many ways but weak and, I think, treacherous. Yet he has breeding and great intellect and sensitivity, and of course he is most attractive, which makes up for a lot!

Walking back through the beechwoods in the rain and the intense quiet we suddenly stopped and our eyes met. We searched each other's faces. Gently he kissed my forehead and my neck. Then with an abrupt movement he was down in the mud at my feet, kneeling and embracing my knees. After that I was done for, I was in his arms at last, and kissing him with all my strength. He broke away and looked at me with a kind of wonder in his eyes, a pain. They were very large and dark, shadowy and yet luminous. His hair fell over his forehead and over his eyes and he looked strange and wonderful in the green light of the woods.

'You are marvellous,' he hissed in my ear. 'You are exciting and so strong and kind. And you are clever too –' he laughed, showing his white animal's teeth – 'really clever and yet you say nothing. Like the silver birch you are exciting because nobody knows what you are thinking.'

With my back against the tree as if I were crucified I held him hard and returned his kisses until the wood had grown dark. He loosened his coat so that I could put my arms around him and feel his thin ribs through his shirt. I kissed his hair, his forehead, with the deep line between the eyes that I'd longed to kiss since I first saw him. As we walked back in the moonlight, black silhouettes, Zoltan was a shadow of an apostle – probably Judas.

'You,' he said, 'look like a naughty boy. Will you grow your hair after the war?' As we waited at the bus stop, he got in a parting shot. 'Does Petya read *Faust* to you?'

'Oh yes, all the time.'

'And say, "If I could say unto the passing moment stay awhile, thou art so fair"? And play you the C minor quartet?'

'Of course – non-stop.'

'Ha ha!' Zoltan said with relish. 'He plays the same tricks for all his girls. But don't be afraid, *I'm* not playing with you. I feel I've known you for years and years and I will never harm you. I just want to see you again and again and again. Will you tell Petya about us?'

'Yes,' I said, 'I'll tell him when he rings tomorrow.'

We parted at the bus stop with Zoltan muttering about 'going home alone in the wind, the dark and the storm'. Till I pointed out that the rain had stopped and it was now a fine bright night.

The bus came all too soon – pushing up the sleeve of my raincoat he kissed the inside of my arm, sending a thrill right through me.

'I'll ring you tomorrow,' he said and was gone.

Thursday, 20th

Needless to say he didn't ring (apparently I had given him the wrong telephone number), but I had no time to worry about it. On the 19th we raided Dieppe, with intense fighter activity over France, and for eight hours at a stretch we were never off the table. I was drenched with sweat, my hands so damp and shaking I could hardly put down the arrows. Our losses were terribly high, nearly a hundred planes lost. The only big success was scored by that hero of our girlish dreams, Commando Leader Lord Lovat, who is quite fiendishly debonair and handsome. He and his men destroyed a coastal battery. Tessa has his picture from the *Daily Mirror* pinned up over her bed.

Saturday, 22nd

Zoltan didn't ring or write for a whole week. Then at last a wire came, a good 4s. 6d. worth, most impressing to someone like me who tends to write almost unintelligible wires for economy reasons.

He says he has been writing letters and tearing them up and how happy he was with me in the woods and perhaps we can see each other next week.

Needless to say I have said nothing to Petya.

Tuesday, 25th

Three nights later the blow fell. I found a note waiting for me in the Filter Room. It informed me that I was posted to Windermere for a two-weeks' refresher course and after that to Inverness. I was flabbergasted.

The Bedstead took me aside for a little chat. 'You see, Wyndham, we have nothing personal against you in this Mess, but you just don't seem to be up to the work here at present. You moon around most of the time, and take no part in service activities, and frankly your mind seems to be permanently elsewhere!'

Of course she's absolutely right, I haven't been pulling my weight at all lately. The course will be mostly the same old thing, brushing up on our Filtering techniques, plus a bit of admin (pregnant aircraftwomen, VD, etc.) and a dose of square-bashing. After that, duly chastened, I'm to be banished to Inverness – the end of the world – where they probably feel I can do least damage. There's only one consoling thought, I shall be with Pandora and Oscar again. What bliss after the awful, stuck-up girls here.

Nevertheless, the posting came as a bit of a shock. I wired Zoltan in despair and rang up Petya, arranging to see him tomorrow.

Wednesday, 26th

Arrived at Petya's studio, shaking with nerves. We talked about the weather. Strangely enough, my departure for Scotland didn't seem to worry him as much as I had thought it would. I sat and drank cocoa, he slashed away feverishly with pastels at his worktable. Suddenly he jumped up and came to face me.

'You're not much of an actress, are you? And I'm no good at pretending. Let's have a showdown, shall we, about Zoltan?'

So he had known ever since Saturday night, when he saw my eyes and knew, he had actually known on that night when he was saying those marvellous things to me, and I had thought him a poor dupe. He had known, and got a kick out of it!

'Oh yes,' he said, 'that night was wonderful, incredible, the irony of it was magnificent and don't forget, my dear, my innate taste for drama. But that irony! It runs in my family, you've only got to look at the line at the corner of my father's mouth. No wonder I love Goethe's *Faust* above everything else in literature! I suppose you've been seeing Zoltan? Oh well, if you think he'll make you happy, go ahead. After all, he must appear to you as the answer to all your dreams. Do you know why I was taking the trouble to instruct you in the correct methods of sexual intercourse the other night? Just in case you should make a fool of yourself with Zoltan and because I have an eye to your future!'

What an incredible creature! I felt weak with amazement.

'However,' Petya went on, 'I must warn you that Zoltan is interested in no one but himself, so he may not even have noticed what was written all over your face. But I saw it and I want your answer.'

I told him – I hardly know what – vague protestations and half-denials, not even knowing myself what I felt.

'I should also warn you,' he continued, 'that everything about Zoltan is false, a façade only. He only wanted you for his butterfly collection. And the fact that he was pinching you from me would only have added spice to the pursuit.'

His eyes were bright and very blue. 'Just kiss me once more, for goodbye. I get such a thrill from your kisses. I don't know why – you don't kiss particularly well. So kiss me quickly, before the wind blows the petals from the roof. What's it matter whether you mean it or not?'

I kissed him very tenderly, and we said goodbye.

'Thank you again for Saturday night,' he said as we went down the stairs. 'I really loved you for lying to me so cruelly and in-nocently. It's only irony like that that makes a woman lastingly beautiful. By the way, you might be interested to know when I first realised that Zoltan intended to seduce you. It was when I saw him standing by the window and saying that your drawings were good, and that of course was a lie. Your drawings are lousy, they are terrible! I never thought that Zoltan would lie about art, how-ever much he wanted a woman.'

I had hardly entered the Mess when the phone rang and it was

Zoltan in a terrible state over my posting, demanding that I see him immediately. We met in Piccadilly Underground. I was wearing my red brigand's cap and Zoltan came late, rushing in with his coat over his shoulders, and kissed the palm of my hand murmuring, 'I love your hat. It looks wonderful.'

We said goodbye in Windsor Park, and walked down a long avenue of trees towards the equestrian statue – strangely unreal, with the dark rearing horse and a pallid rainbow over the cornfields.

We lay under a tree in the wind and the rain eating peaches while Zoltan kissed my thighs with his usual air of grave, sad absorption. He undid his shirt so that I could put my hand over his heart, and the wind roared in the trees and whipped back my hair.

He said slowly, 'Joan, I wish you were my wife.' I couldn't speak because I felt like crying. He asked if I were an angel or a devil, and I told him I was one of those that Dante writes of who are neither for God nor against him, but for 'themselves alone'.

'Ah, I see you're clever too – that's interesting! Not too bloody clever though, or you wouldn't have fallen for a bastard like me who will undoubtedly ruin your life.'

Walking back I was light-headed from lack of sleep and clung to his sleeve while he stopped to pick up a raven's feather and wrote strange things with it on the palm of my hand. He told me I am not just a woman, but a right good chap, which was more important.

On the train going back we kissed in an empty carriage. He wouldn't take me to his flat, he said, in case it would make the thing commonplace.

Tomorrow I go to Windermere. He promises to write daily and ring me all the time. He can't wait to see me on leave – apparently I shall get a few days before my posting to Scotland. My father is lending me his studio in Notting Hill Gate, so we will be alone at last.

28th August

Utter hell! Only thoughts of Zoltan keep me sane. We are in the Belleville Hotel right on Lake Windermere, sleeping in bunks. Every morning at crack of dawn we have to hit the parade ground, and all day long there are lectures in the Nissen huts on how to be an administration officer. Apparently we shall be expected to do quite a bit of admin work in Scotland.

The woman who sleeps under me is an intensely vital ex-social welfare worker who wears a monocle. She drives me mad.

Here is a typical day's programme – parade (and at least four things found wrong with my appearance. 'Ropy do, Wyndham, your collar is filthy!') Then a lecture on VD and scabies, followed by compulsory hockey in a thunderstorm – then another lecture on pregnant WAAFs. As if this wasn't enough we have a compulsory cello concert after dinner – can you imagine, after all that, a *cello* concert?

No letter yet from Zoltan – rang him but no reply.

Sunday, 6th September

Hoped that Zoltan might have rung by now but he hasn't. Last night we went to a wizard dance given by the 18th Hussars and I got very drunk on jungle juice. The hussars were fighting like wolves to dance with me. I don't know their real names but there was Mutt, Jeff, Whiskers, Pimples and Impedimento, who talks as if he has a mouthful of chestnuts.

All are hot on my trail, and they ring the hotel leaving little notes saying, 'How about blowing up to C Mess tomorrow night for a spot of wine, waltz and what-have-you?' It's the what-have-you that I'm worried about because I can't be interested in any man except Zoltan.

I've written twice. Why doesn't he answer? Our leave together has been all arranged.

Tuesday, 8th

Now that the weather is fine the lake is really lovely. It's smooth and transparent as glass with pine trees and mountains and little feathery islands like a Japanese print.

There is only one decent type in my room, a cheery and vulgar girl much given to 'scrubbing around' parades she doesn't fancy. There is a rude song going around the Mess at the moment which starts, 'There goes m'daughter sir, Can't 'old 'er water sir.' Well, this girl has the same disability, and had an awful accident during the Commanding Officer's lecture on 'The Moral Aspect'. We have christened her Wee Wee White.

Big speech from Churchill today, mostly about Africa and Rommel. He's sending Alexander and Monty there to sort him out. Apart from that all the news is a bit depressing – lots of our convoys are being sunk, and the Germans are surrounding Stalingrad.

Today I have written to Zoltan again. His silence is beginning to make me feel rather ill.

Tonight I am definitely going to ring him up come what may.

Thursday, 10th

It's very strange. Last night I rang him three times. Each time a foreign woman answered and I put the phone down. I feel very upset and don't quite know what to do. I've written to him four times over the last two weeks and still no answer.

As today was our last day we went to this marvellous hotel called the Waterside at Ambleside, and everyone drank champagne and tucked into fresh salmon and home-made trifle but I couldn't eat a thing. I felt miserable and strangely feverish. My leave starts tomorrow – it's all fixed up for me to have Daddy's studio in Bedford Gardens – and still no sign from Zoltan.

Friday, 11th

I'm going to London to look for Zoltan. I don't know if I shall find him, but if I don't I think I shall go mad.

The train is coming into the slums and factories now. I'd be scared as hell if I let myself go.

I rang again from the station – again a woman answered, so I took a taxi to my father's studio in Bedford Gardens, changed, had a bath and explored the premises.

Every drawer seems filled with contraceptives, Benzedrine, or Luminal sleeping tablets. And there's a box of aphrodisiacs called 'Dr Parker's Satyricon Cachets', and something called 'Herculeian Tabloids'. Even better, there's a sideboard stocked with gin, vermouth, whisky, and some flat champagne. It is a weird and gloomy studio with a draped surrealist lay figure and a huge sunlamp.

After my bath I set off for the Grampians where Zoltan lives – a huge block of flats. The lift is one of those new kind where you press the button yourself and watch the floor numbers slowly sinking past you. It was No. 7 and the flat was on a balcony that ran along the side of the block, high up over the misty houses where lights were just beginning to show. It seemed like a dream that I should be really there.

I knocked on the door but no one came. I looked at the letter-box and looked through and saw Zoltan's grey and black tweed coat hanging on the wall. I remembered that coat covering me in the woods at Windsor. Well at least he was still in residence.

Sadly I went back to the studio and as I was walking along the grey, gloomy corridor, dreading the night to come, I heard music coming from an open door, and a low cheerful buzz that warmed my heart. As I hesitated outside, a tall young man with a white face popped his head round the corner.

'Hello,' he said, 'I'm Hector – do you know the Roberts?'

'Who?' I said.

'Colquhoun and McBryde, of course, our genial hosts. They're giving a party for Johnny Minton who's on leave.' Then he looked at my face and said, 'God, you look dreadful! You'd better come in and have a drink.'

50

There were lots of bottles all over the room and a long table covered with food, mostly salads and herrings fried in oatmeal. Unfortunately someone had cut their finger opening a can of beer and there was blood all over the herrings. Feeling ravenous, I found a reasonably clean one and wolfed it down. A little hunchback woman was going round pouring drinks and she gave me some wine cup. I felt almost drunk already from the sheer relief of being with people again.

'That piss is nae guid!' a Scottish voice said, 'Hae some whuskey!' It turned out to be one of the Roberts, hollow-cheeked and handsome in a wolfish sort of way, and wearing a bright red jersey. He put the wet mouth of his bottle to my lips and I took a long gulp. It went down like fire. He took a swig himself, leapt into the centre of the room, threw out his arms and began to recite with demonic energy and wild dramatic gestures:

> Clerk Sanders and May Margret
> walked o'er yon gravelled green
> and sad and heavy was the love
> that fell this twa between.
> A bed, a bed! Clerk Sanders said —

'Good stuff, isn't it,' Hector said, steering me towards a little back room, 'come and meet some other people. That's Paul Potts, the People's Poet, the pretty dark one with the funny teeth is Johnny Minton the painter and the old bear in the armchair reading Burns is Hugh McDiarmid, another poet.'

McDiarmid raised his craggy head and spat out a few incomprehensible lines in Lallan Scots, before lapsing back into a glowering silence. I tried talking to him about Burns but he hooted with sardonic laughter and said, 'Ye dinna understan' oot, ye ramfeezled hizzy,' or some such Scottish rudery, so I felt it was time to move on.

I was aware of Hector's arm around my shoulders, a bottle being held to my lips — whisky I think. I was getting drunker every minute and Zoltan seemed a million miles away.

The other Robert, smaller and merrier than his friend, drew us into a circle and we danced to a children's song: 'Water, water, wild flower, growing up so high. We are all children and we must all die.'

The white-faced boy with buck teeth leapt into the middle, cavorting like a rag doll. 'Except Johnny Minton, the fairest of them all!' chanted the circling dancers.

By now the room was spinning round me. Far in the distance I could hear Colquhoun's voice – 'Oh fair Margret, and rare Margret, and Margret o' memorie.' My eyes grew dim and I slumped to the floor.

When I woke up I was back in my father's studio, lying in bed fully clothed, and a man, naked except for a black mackintosh, was standing at the end of my bed. I leapt up terrified but he said, 'Don't be frightened – it's me, Hector. I only need somewhere to kip for the night.' So saying he threw off the mac and dived under the blankets. Fully awake now and almost sober, I began to clamber out of the other side of the bed, but he pulled me back.

'Don't be alarmed, I'm not going to touch you. In fact, to be quite honest I've never had a woman in my life. Christ, I could use another drink. You don't have any around, do you?'

I indicated my dad's well-stocked bar. He helped himself liberally to a gin, poured in some vermouth and sat naked on the edge of the bed. 'You see,' he went on, 'I'm madly in love with this orthodox Jewish girl, and she wants me to be a virgin when I marry her. I've got some other problems too – are you sure you wouldn't like a drink?'

'Gosh no, I'm practically in an alcoholic stupor already. But what are your other problems?'

'Well,' Hector continued, 'there was this German governess I had when I was five. She was blonde and beautiful and very sadistic, and she wore a black shiny mackintosh. Every morning she used to beat me and give me an enema. Naturally I was madly in love with her, and ever since then all these things have been a positive mania with me. You don't happen to have a whip handy, do you? Or an enema, perhaps? You see, I've got the black mackintosh so it would be quite handy.'

'No, I'm afraid I haven't any of those,' I said, hardly able to believe my ears.

'Oh well, never mind, I'm pretty whacked actually and I've got to work tomorrow. D'you mind if I get in again? I promise you nothing will happen.'

In fact, I was so frightened of being alone that I quite welcomed his company and next morning we breakfasted off Benzedrine and flat champagne. What a funny spectacle, the girl who tries everything once! My heart began to beat about twice as fast as usual. I could almost hear it. At the same time my body seemed to be made of taut live wires, my face was stiff with tension and my fists clenched. I had never tried Benzedrine before and it certainly had a weird effect on me.

Hector turns out to be a reporter on the *Sunday Graphic*. He asked me to go dancing with him at the Studio Club later, but I said there was someone I had to see, someone I'd come to London to look for. Hector looked dashed and lit a cigar.

'Oh well,' he said, 'I'll be at Prunier's about eight o'clock, and if this bloke doesn't materialise you can join me there.'

I spent a terrible day, sitting in front of the popping gas-fire and waiting for six o'clock when I thought Zoltan would be back from work, smoking innumerable cigarettes and trying to read Huxley. My forefinger was stained brown with nicotine, the colour of the thin brown fog outside the studio window.

Walking to the Grampians I could feel it permeating my hair, making my eyes sting, seeping into the bomb craters and the gaps between houses. Nearly a year now since we were bombed, but the ruins are still there to remind us.

I climbed the stairs to his flat and sat on the floor in the dark, leaning my head against the door in the freezing cold. Through other doors I could hear happy voices, smell dinners being cooked. Suddenly someone stepped out of Zoltan's flat, a woman, her high heels tapping on the concrete. I sat within an inch of her, in the dark, but couldn't speak, feeling sick with jealousy and frustration. After she had gone I left, and took a taxi to Prunier's where Hector was waiting for me.

'You win,' I said and started to tell him about Zoltan. When I came to the episode in Windsor Park he said, 'With or without a mackintosh?' and left it at that.

Manhattans to start with – then two dozen oysters, lobster à l'Américaine, brandy mousse and a couple of cigars for Hector, who behaved belligerently throughout as befits a Communist paying £3-odd for a simple meal. He kept complaining that the waiters weren't treating him with sufficient deference because his clothes were shabby.

Then back to the Studio Club, a dreary cellar with awful paintings on the walls, where we danced and drank cherry brandy. It was Free French night, packed with sailors and *poilus* and lovely girls in black satin dresses with gold crosses round their necks.

I had taken quite a few of my father's pills and my head felt as if it were packed with cotton wool. The fat man at the piano was playing 'Skylark'; the music was sad and beautiful, but my main fear was that Hector would want to go to bed with me. But he was so nice and kind, knowing that I was unhappy, that I told him he could come provided it was only to sleep. After all it was raining and the last tube had gone.

I find him quite attractive in a sinister sort of way, with his dead-white bony face, and hair that flops over his forehead, but there's something strange and obsessive about him which frightens me. He carries pornographic prints around in his briefcase – and all that stuff about black mackintoshes and enemas! Apparently he's quite good at his job, but has to be a bit careful what he writes as he's a raging Communist, which is not a popular point of view even if the Russkies *are* our allies!

We went home declaiming loudly to the stars about atheism and free love, lit the geyser, washed and then went to bed together. I took three tablets of Hypneural and lay down beside him in my dressing-gown. I was dead asleep in a few minutes. Next morning, before it was light, he woke and tried to force me, saying, 'Wouldn't you like to seduce a virgin?' I fought him for what seemed like hours. In the end I was so tired I gave in. He soon became very passionate, and each orgasm seemed to knock him out and exhaust him completely. Later he lay awake till five telling me about his Jewish girlfriend.

I (as usual) had felt absolutely nothing. Hector simply refused to believe me when I told him this. 'With a mouth like that?' he asked.

What shamed me beyond everything was the fact that I'd felt no differently with a stranger than I had with someone I loved; it was almost exactly the same. What is this love then that I have so fondly believed in? Has it never existed as a thing apart, and is it purely a chemical result of the physical embrace? It is a dreadful thought.

I felt that in some way this was the lowest hour of my life – but then some part of me that had escaped and hidden in a cave began sending me strange thoughts, blue as a spring day, cool and very bright. Childhood, Christmas, my mother – peace, rest and normality and then at last the consolation of tears. I lay in his arms and cried silently and unceasingly, my tears falling on his hand.

The sun was rising and a cold grey light began to fill the room. Soon it was light enough for us to turn and look at one another. He looked at my tears, and I at his forehead which smoked like a wood fire in the frosty air, strange and beautiful. He tried to comfort me by saying, 'You're very brave and good and I'm a beast and a pig. What you need is a proper husband and proper children.'

Then he got up and lit the fire and brought me a glass of wine in bed. It glowed in the first rays of the sun which were swimming with dust motes. 'You look weird and fey,' Hector said, 'like something that's come out of the mist.' In fact I felt rather like an ageing and passé tart after an unsuccessful night's trade. Another three glasses of wine, then I lent him £2 and sent him on his way.

By six o'clock I was back at the Grampians, and at the very height of my madness. Drugged and drunk as usual, I dodged maids, doormen and tenants, crouching at the turnings of stone stairs, whizzing up and down in the lift, peering over into Zoltan's window from the balcony above. I felt like a thief or a spy.

Finally I plucked up enough courage to knock on his door. It was opened by a woman in a dressing-gown. 'Zoltan has been away in the country,' she said, 'I've no idea when he'll be back. Why do you want to see him?' I gave her a note – 'Please ring Park 7887 as soon as you get home' – and ran away quickly to escape her curiosity.

Back in the studio I lit the fire and drank two glasses of neat whisky, then lay down on the bed in my hat and coat. The next thing I knew it was morning, my coat was crumpled and the light was still burning. Zoltan had not rung. My last hope, my last link with him was Petya – I took three Benzedrine and got up enough courage to ring him.

I thought his voice sounded strange on the phone but he seemed glad to hear from me and asked me to come round that evening. With the rest of the day to kill, I walked over to the Mercury Theatre to see *Hedda Gabler* which I found intensely exciting. Then at six I walked through the rain to Petya's house. The door was open and I climbed the stairs. He came out suddenly on to the landing and his face lit up when he saw me.

'Are you drunk?' he said.

'No,' I said, 'just a bit dopey.'

He kissed me and there was silence for a moment. Then he said in a quiet strained voice, 'You are in for a surprise – there is a mutual friend of ours upstairs.'

My feet stumbled and I swayed from side to side going up the stairs. There are three flights, very dark, and then at the top the landing with the lighted door opening on to it.

A figure was leaning in the doorway, a black shape against the white glare of the lamp from the studio. I kept my eyes fixed on it, fighting to control myself and holding hard on to the banisters. On the last step Zoltan's voice said 'Joan' and his fingers were unbuttoning my coat and he was holding my hand and saying, 'How cold and wet your hands are – where have you been all this time?' I couldn't look at him but I kept myself turned towards Petya as if for protection, and answered him like a sleepwalker.

Inside were a lot of clever girls in corduroy trousers, a few young artists, an elderly social worker, a tongue-tied young soldier in battledress and a former prime minister of Hungary who appeared to suffer from a cleft palate. They must have all thought me mad, because I couldn't speak or even see them properly but wandered in looking pale and distraught with wet hair hanging over my eyes, and sat down by the fire.

Zoltan came and sat on the floor beside me. We hardly spoke a word. When I asked how he had been he said, 'Very bad,' and smiled his slow, mocking smile.

Then we were all shepherded into the next room. Petya played – inevitably – the C minor quartet. Zoltan stood by the wall, his hands over his eyes. There was some talk of the war, the attacks on Russian convoys, our raid on Tobruk, the fighting on the outskirts of Stalingrad, but most people seemed more interested in the relation of art to science.

I noticed that Petya behaved in a very feminine way towards Zoltan throughout the evening, putting his hand on his shoulder and saying, 'Well, here we have an expert!' removing something – a thread of cotton, perhaps – from his beard, and pressing his hand and smiling at him. In his heart does he really hate him – this worst friend that anyone ever had?

When Zoltan left I left with him and soon we were walking down the middle of the road arm in arm. There were no sirens – we had not had a raid on London for ages – and I felt happy and secure. He was wearing a red scarf and a black beret and he looked so handsome and kind that all my worries fell away from me.

'It is so pleasant, Joan, walking in the rain with you – it is a luxury I cannot afford.'

I asked him why he had not written to me, why he hadn't rung. I told him just a little of my unhappiness, but he could only say that things had become terrible and he had not known what to do. That he'd been in trouble with the police, his wife was ill, he owed money and so on. He seemed surprised that I had been so miserable, and felt dreadfully guilty about it. The woman in the flat, he explained, was just an aunt of his called Tigreed. Apparently she was much impressed by me, I was so young, and so insistent! Which didn't answer the painful question of why he had not responded to my note. But all I could do was cling to his arm and say nothing, just hoping that he wasn't going to leave me again.

At the door of the studio he said, 'I think I must say goodnight now.'

My heart fell like a stone. I pleaded without shame for him to come in and after a little resistance he did.

I poured him a huge drink and lit the gas-fire, but he didn't even take his coat off.

'I must go soon,' he said when he had tossed back the whisky. 'I'm not good for you, I don't wish to disturb your peace.'

'You have already disturbed it as much as possible.'

'Ah no, I could disturb you infinitely more. I could break you, and I wouldn't want to do that.'

Then he suddenly laid his head in my lap and I bent and kissed him and we were in each other's arms and soon I was lying beside him on the bed.

We turned out the light and talked of death, how he could die with me, but never live with me.

'I will kill you, and then kill myself. Would you let me, Joan? How would you like to die? Shall I strangle you?'

I almost wished he had meant it instead of merely indulging a favourite pose – at least he may not be posing, but there is a lot of difference between wanting and a cold resolution to take action.

It was lovely to have him in my arms, but I remember so little of it. Why can't I remember every detail, every minute? Suddenly he turned and said, 'Have you been with a man, Joan? You have, haven't you?'

'Yes,' I said, wondering how he had known. 'You see, I was so lonely and miserable.'

'Ah, Joan, you are a monster. You are a terrible, immoral creature. Who was he? What is his name? Did he sleep with you here, in this bed? Will he come again? Ah, Joan, how strange, how you have changed! I find you deeply abused, deeply degenerated and deeply spoilt – and you are only twenty. You are very young to have been hurt so much.'

And all the time he was talking he was kissing and caressing me and muttering to himself, 'How strange.' The rain lashed the windows and we listened to it remembering how it was always raining or dark or cold when we were together. He tried to undo my stockings and I said very levelly, 'Would you prefer me to take off my clothes instead of fumbling with those suspenders?'

'Joan! Do not use that professional tone! You are not a whore – yet – though you could have a great talent in that direction, you know. You do not get excited. Tell me, are you a whore? But no, you are a fearful, moral creature.'

I knew by then that he would sleep with me. I took my clothes off and he covered me with the rug and lay beside me. He said, kissing me, 'You have the most beautiful breasts. I should really go, my dearest, but you're such a lovely creature, so what can I do? I think in this light I love you.'

'In this light' – how cruelly frank are these men we love.

He took off his clothes. All men look undignified when they're undressing, even Zoltan, so elegant and distinguished. My last thought as he took me in his arms was that I'd taken no precautions and I didn't care. I must give some sort of a hostage to fortune.

It was better with him than with anyone else, he was completely detached, very gentle and sad and very much afraid that he would hurt me.

Afterwards he asked me if he had given me any shadow of pleasure, and I told him yes, more than a shadow.

'And I felt none – how strange that is.'

We lay for a long time in each other's arms and I sighed very deeply because at last I was completely happy. As if he resented my happiness and was determined to destroy it he immediately got up off the bed. 'Listen to the rain. I suppose I'd better be off soon.' I went cold with shock, and asked why he couldn't stay, but he only sighed and said that the morning would be unbearable for both of us. When he had finished dressing he stood by the bed looking down at me. 'Being with you is like being with a ghost, and ghosts don't survive daylight. This is the only possible ending, that I should walk home through the rain.' He leant down and kissed my forehead. 'I shall never see you again, Joan.'

Oh the sickness, the cold misery that came over me, because at that moment I was not strong enough to bear it. Turning my head into the pillow I cried with hard sobs of despair. He put his head close to mine and hissed into my ear, almost with hatred, 'Joan! Surely you're not like that? So what will you do now? Kill yourself? Shall I bring you poison to take, like my wife?'

No words can describe the gentle brutality of his words and voice. I froze into stillness, and taking my hand from his lay there with the tears drying up in my eyes. An astonishing change came over him – his eyes lit up with weary pleasure.

'And have I succeeded in offending you at last? Tell me, have I? I tried hard enough, in all truth, didn't I?'

'Yes, yes,' I cried, almost sobbing and very tired.

'I'm glad that I've won,' he said, and left me.

After he had gone I slept so peacefully. Now that the tension, the uncertainty was gone, I no longer cared whether he broke me or not or even whether he left me or not. I no longer cared if I ever saw him again.

My last day in the studio

At dawn I woke slowly and painfully, and the full impact of the last few days hit me between the eyes. I moaned aloud and turned back into my pillows. Hours later I got up, put on my dressing-gown and got drunk. Then lay beside the gas-fire for three or four hours. I couldn't control my thoughts, they beat and harried me without rest, but I knew beyond any doubt that I had to forget Zoltan and wipe him from my memory.

With a deep sigh I got up and looked at my face in the ward-robe mirror — is that really me? I'm much thinner and my eyes have a curious clouded, oblique look. I'm very pale. You poor bloody fool, I said, what have you done to yourself? Then I took three Benzedrine — silly, ludicrous ape of a creature! A strange feeling of calm came over me as I lay in the bath, lis-tening to the wireless talking about Stalingrad. How remote the war seems to me just now. Then I dressed and went over to Petya's place.

'You've come just in time,' he exclaimed, not seeming at all surprised to see me. 'I'm doing this poster for the French Government and I need someone to pose for the sniper. Take off your clothes and grab this umbrella.'

'But why should a sniper have no clothes on?'

'No reason at all, it just makes it more fun for me.'

Petya seemed in excellent mood for someone who had just lost his best girl and his best friend.

Crouching naked, umbrella in hand, I told him that Zoltan and I were not going to see each other any more.

'Good,' Petya said. 'That's the best news I've heard in a long time — provided, of course, you mean it. Incidentally, you do realise he's a complete bastard, don't you?' he went on, splashing red blood over a dead German. 'Why do you think he never took you back to his place?'

60

'Well, he said he didn't want to make our relationship commonplace.'

'Commonplace! My poor dear girl, the reason he didn't take you back was because his fifty-five-year-old mistress was there. Tigreed gives him a hard time, but she also gives him a bit of money.'

'I see, so it wasn't his aunt! — but why didn't he write.'

'Same reason, you were causing complications. Zoltan can't really afford a grand romantic gesture. As for all that nonsense he talked to you about love — a fraud, just a façade. He rather fancies you as another feather in his cap, especially if he can nick it out of mine.'

I was feeling more and more depressed and also getting cramp in my right leg but Petya was remorseless.

'What else did he tell you about himself, as a matter of interest?'

'Well, he said he hadn't long to live because of stomach cancer.'

Petya snorted with laughter. 'Cirrhosis of the liver possibly — syphilis, perhaps — but *not* stomach cancer! What an incurably gullible romantic you are, my poor girl.'

After he had finished painting he sent me out to get meat and onions for a stew, which I cooked for him, putting in plenty of paprika. Both of us by now are feeling unaccountably cheerful, in fact I found I liked Petya much better now that he was no longer so romantic about me.

While we ate I told him all about my search for Zoltan — my phone calls and the note I left for him. Petya was horrified.

'Women don't *do* these things!' he exclaimed. 'You should never have left that note for Zoltan. When a man feels that a woman is pursuing him, he is disgusted. Do you realise that I had to watch Zoltan take your note out of his pocket when he was in my studio and say sneeringly, 'Joan has asked me to ring her, but I shall not do it.' And when I said you were coming later he declared that he would leave before you arrived. You should never have put yourself into such a position, it was too humiliating.'

I had brought over a bottle pinched from my dad's studio and soon we became mellow, affectionate, almost happy. Petya swore he would stick by me and always be my best friend. While I was modelling for the victim of a Careless Talk poster, with strawberry jam coming out of my mouth, he asked me how my dreams were getting on. I told him that last night I dreamt I was marrying the Pope. 'You're a hopeless case,' Petya said. 'I think you really ought to see a psychiatrist.'

Later we went down to the Swiss to try and find Dylan Thomas who owed him £5, but he wasn't there so we went to a little Portuguese shop in the Charing Cross Road and Petya bought me some sex hormones.

'Now you really know I'm your friend,' he said. 'By the time these work you'll be miles away and surrounded by randy Scottish pilots. What's more,' he went on, 'I'll even carry your bags to the station tomorrow.'

There was only one thing more I wanted to do before I left for Scotland, and that was to see Rupert again. I knew he had been invalided out and was back in London so I went round on the off-chance.

As usual, he was in bed, but he was delighted to see me and got up to make me some tea.

'Christ, Joan,' he said, 'you look too bad to be true, what have you been doing, doping yourself?'

I told him about the Benzedrine and the Hypneural and he said, 'What you really need is something called Sedormid, I'll give you some of mine. That'll calm you down and you'll be able to dangle the world at arm's length on a piece of string in no time. How do you think I survived the Navy?'

Nevertheless, he thought I looked very smart in my uniform and was most impressed that I no longer bit my nails.

'God! Just look at your nails,' he said. 'You're getting to be quite a *femme du monde*, Joanie.'

After lunch he talked to me so wisely and sanely and cheerfully about Petya and Zoltan. He's very amused at me for being so impressed with pseudo-intellectuals, and can hardly believe that I actually talk about 'great artists'. He thinks it's just a phase and that I ought to marry someone sane and steady and settle down. I feel that he's the best friend I've ever had and the most real person, the one I still feel closest to. And now he belongs to Annie and not me any more.

Nevertheless we lay underneath the black and white rug in the semi-darkness and I rested my head on his shoulder, and he leant his cheek against my hair and we talked just like we used to do in Redcliffe Road in the old days – about sex, mostly, and the funny things women do, and Jaffa oranges and custard tarts and Pooh Bear and how his mum can still hear mice squeaking in her wooden leg, and he advised me to go and see Dr Danzigen about my frigidity and get some passion pills, like Prudey did.

BOOK III

Wednesday, 16th September

INVERNESS

On the night train to Inverness I raised the shade at dawn and saw a white horse with mane streaming, racing the train. Then just before Pitlochry the sun illumined a broad river plumed with mist under the dark hills, with big birds scavenging in the dried-up shallows.

Oscarine and Pandora met me at the station: the sight of their smiling faces was like coming home. I felt I was Eurydice back from a long sojourn in the Underworld.

And there was the town of Inverness, with its reddish stone houses roofed with grey granite, the smoke wafting up into the damp blue air, and Cemetery Hill with its black trees and white marble crosses, the air so clear and soft, and the autumn trees brilliant in the sun, yellow, purple and red by the broad brown river.

It was only a short walk to the WAAF Mess, a grey stone house called the Windsor Hotel with bay windows and a little lawn fronting on to the river.

The room I am going to share with Oscar is lovely and sunny, looking out over the Ness. On a wide windowsill are vases filled with rowan berries.

As I bounced happily on the bed, which seemed extremely

comfortable, Oscar explained about the washing arrangement. 'The bathroom is down the corridor,' she said, 'but the hot water is extremely limited, and you have to be sure to bag it before Gloves does. She spends hours there and uses gallons.'

'Gloves' Galagher is apparently the officer in charge of our Mess. Oscar says she is very handsome in a cold sort of way and has a large red setter. Apparently she is called Gloves because of this habit she has of leaving her leather gloves behind in glamorous places so that she can go back for them the next day and get chatted up by the top brass. So far she's scored with Bomber Command HQ, the Cameron Highlanders, and two battleships. The last one netted her an admiral. It seems she's a bit tricky, so I must watch out.

The girls took me on a grand tour of the Mess. 'This main hall is where we have our parties – look at that amazing central staircase, just perfect for making an impressive entrance!'

'Do you have many parties?'

'We certainly do! We're having one next week. That room on the right with the tatty sofas and the gas-fire is the passion parlour. You can take your boyfriend there on his own if you book it ahead in time. The little back room with the hideous tartan wallpaper is where we eat, and the kitchen is next door, nice and convenient for midnight snacks. You must be starving, I'll make you a cup of tea and some toast, and then we'll explore the islands. That's where the really heavy stuff goes on!'

These are only five minutes' walk from the Mess, wooded isles set in the foaming river Ness and connected by little white bridges. 'You've just no idea what goes on here – it's terribly convenient,' said Oscar as we leant back against a big tree trunk and had a smoke while I caught up on all the news. Oscar is in love with a mad Norwegian sea captain called Danny, but she doesn't see him much as his motor torpedo boat is stationed in the Shetland Isles. Pandora is still a virgin, but she rather fancies a married Canadian major at a nearby camp (bags of Catholic guilt).

Apparently the work here is pretty monotonous, so their eyes came out on stalks when I told them about the mad flaps we had at Stanmore, especially the raid on Dieppe. At the mention of Dieppe Oscar got very excited – apparently Lord Lovat's castle is only a few miles from Inverness and he used to train his commandos in the park. 'We caught a glimpse of him in town,' she said, 'and he's *gorgeous*!'

After that we naturally began to talk about men, and I described Zoltan and Petya. Pandora said she thought Zoltan sounded an awful bore and a dreadful poseur. 'What on earth did you see in him?' she asked. I tried to explain that he had been so handsome, and had said such lovely things.

'The trouble with you is that you're an incurable romantic.'

'Don't I know it! I only wish I could fall in love sensibly and sanely.'

'All I want,' said Pandora, 'is an all-redeeming passion that will swoop down on me and possess me, something to make me totally forget myself – preferably with someone who isn't married.'

'Fat chance,' muttered Oscar. 'Especially with the chaps we've got here. Oh, they're nice clean types all right, but terribly dull, always trying to take us for seven-mile walks. I only really like men who are either highly intellectual or downright vulgar. Come to think of it I've never had a boyfriend who didn't have something wrong with him, either mentally or physically.'

'Me too,' I said.

We lay back listening to the rushing water and lit another cigarette.

Apparently the only decent men around here are the Canadians and the Norwegian sailors on the motor-torpedo boats, but unfortunately the flotilla is not due back from the Shetlands till next year.

'What's so special about *them*?' I asked.

'Only that they're gorgeous, sexy and very, very funny, and they drink like fishes and take over the whole town – it's like a Viking invasion. The one I'm in love with, Danny, is so mad, so brave and so drunken that he frightens his crew even more than the enemy.'

As we strolled back to the Windsor, she pointed out some convenient drainpipes. 'That,' she said, 'is where they climb up to our rooms.'

I must say life here doesn't sound too bad.

The place where we work is up a hill, just out of town. Sometimes we get transport, but mostly we do it on our bikes. You dive underground and come out in a big bright room, much cheerier than Stanmore, in fact the whole atmosphere is more friendly and relaxed. After the hectic dramas down south I may well find myself getting a bit bored with the work up here. All we did on our first day was plot a Catalina escorting a convoy, and track down an errant weather balloon!

Saturday, 19th

To my amazement Zoltan has written to me, a sort of last, dramatic gasp, I suppose. He must have sent it the night I left for Scotland.

'Dear Joan,' he writes, 'I'm sitting at home feeling terribly unreal. You probably sleep and travel through strange landscapes, marvellous shapes and colours, noticing nothing. And you do not even feel the waves of my sea, tender, wild, merciful, evil, tired and strong. (Did you ever feel them?)

Goodnight (or good morning?) dear Joan. And remember!
Yours, Zoltan.'

I tested my heart to see if it felt anything. There was nothing. Whatever happens I must make a new life here. I shall not be writing back to him.

Two weeks later
Friday, 2nd October

To me there is nothing more staggering than the resilience of the human heart. Its powers of recovery are almost embarrassingly swift! Already after two weeks I have regained my peace of mind. I find myself singing as I run upstairs and I am putting on weight again. Much as I would like to languish and waste away for a bit longer, nature just won't put up with such nonsense.

Of course I miss Petya and Zoltan and even Rupert, but it is so beautiful here and I have good friends, and the work is less hectic so it no longer frightens me.

I've come to realise that Petya's barrage of drama and intensity forced me into an illusion of love which vanished as soon as I left him. My love for Zoltan too was pretty unreal. Now, thank God, I'm nobody's 'soul's image', just a normal, healthy, happy person.

For the first time in my life I am living without fear or anxieties – without excitement too – just peace and rest, friendship and books. I think in time I might become frightfully bored!

Meantime, with my twenty-first birthday coming up, I have sent Mama some crafty hints about presents.

Darling Mama,

Here is a list of things I wouldn't mind for my twenty-first birthday. They are all small things. Of course what I really wanted was a typewriter but I don't think you can get them nowadays. So instead, any of the following – a Brownie No. 2. Stockings, size 10. (Urgently needed, none to be got here. Mine are full of holes! Lillywhites might have them but they are very scarce.) *The Science of Life*, by Wells-Huxley. Coty's 'Vertige' from the Maison Française, if they have any left – otherwise some Coty 'Jasmine Brilliantine'. A black chenille snood, with a bow on top. Some unrationed lace from Bourne and Hollingsworth. Laforgue's poems (try Foyles). Needless to say, anything to eat, chockies particularly welcome!

I've just had my front teeth out – agony but the new ones are *très chic*, if a bit cleaner-looking than their neighbours. Dare say they'll tone down in time.

Just read a book on contact lenses and I'm saving up for some. I should have the necessary say in about six months. The fittings and lenses cost £22 together, from a place in Cavendish Square. As they are made of plastic they are unbreakable. How wonderful it would be not to wear glasses any more!

Well I think that's all for now except that I think I will become a schoolmistress after the war — that is, if I don't get married. Just think how nice to have those long holidays, and teach Eng. Lit. to horrid little girls who get crushes on you. (Actually Oscar and I think up a new profession every week — it's great fun.)

Lots of love,
Joan

Saturday, 3rd

It seems I needn't have worried about being bored! Excitement has arrived in the shape of an invitation to a dance given by the Royal Engineers. What is more it is being held in their Mess at Beaufort Castle, home of Lord Lovat — Commando Leader and hero of the Dieppe beaches. There is not a girl in our Mess who doesn't secretly lust after him — including me! — and the very thought of visiting his home and maybe catching a glimpse of him thrills me to the marrow.

Sunday, 4th

It was a wizard party. I was jitterbugging madly with a French Canadian who danced like an angel when the side door flew open and in came a tall boy in tweeds, about six feet two and bursting out of his much-too-small jacket. I thought he looked a bit of a bounder — whenever you see a man in civvies at one of these do's you immediately think he's the Clerk of Works, or the GPO, and you avoid him like the plague.

However, he began to monopolise me like mad, and my first shock came when he mentioned that he was a Major and had just come back from fighting in Africa. He was only twenty-five and quite handsome with a big hawk-like nose.

The real bombshell was to come. We were sitting out a dance

and I was burbling happily on about this mouldering old dump and what a decadent lot the aristocracy were – the exception, of course, being that wild madcap Lord Lovat, whom I would dearly love to meet. 'There's a rumour he might be coming to the dance,' I twittered on, 'in which case I would be more than ready to lie flat on the floor and let him walk over me in his rubber-soled plimsolls.'

'Oh,' says the boy, 'd'you mean that stinkah Shimi?'

'Why yes. D'you know him?'

'Tolerably well, he is m'cousin, and this mouldering old pile is where I'm spending m'leave.'

Imagine my shame and horror! However, Hamish, for that was the boy's name, thought it all a huge joke and we got drunk together and I was on top form and happy as hell.

We found we had practically every taste in common from Hemingway, flamenco, and bullfights to John Donne and Carnet de Bal, and what's more we are both Catholics.

I asked him where he would be posted to next, but he clammed up. 'You're on Special Duties yourself,' he said, 'you ought to know better than to ask silly questions like that!' So I suppose he's about to do something top secret – how exciting! As for Shimi, his comings and goings are shrouded in even deeper mystery. I suppose if we ever get round to invading France he and his commandos will be among the first on the beaches.

We asked the band to play our favourite tunes and staggered round, followed by furiously jealous glances from all my friends. The REs are a stuffy lot, and I had the best-looking man in the room. Of course, none of them knew who he was, he had just sneaked in from a house-party at the lodge, to see if there was any fun to be had.

About 2 a.m. the lights were turned out and we sang the REs' special song. You go round in a circle doing weird gestures and the Colonel sits in the middle with a lighted lantern. I don't know what it all meant but it sounded fine.

By this time the Hon. Hamish was getting amorous and suggesting we meet on his next leave and stay at the Berkeley, so I thought it was time to go.

Tuesday, 6th

A strange coincidence – Lady Lovat suddenly discovers she knows Pandora's father – and would she come to lunch tomorrow at the castle and bring her nice friend Miss Wyndham?

Obviously there has been some hokey-pokey by the Hon. Hamish and between them they have 'looked me up' and found that I pass muster. So tomorrow off I go in civvies to knock his eye out. With any luck Lord Lovat, pride of the *Daily Mirror*, will be there too.

The whole of the Windsor Hotel is mad with excitement, they say it is awfully promising, just like the opening chapters of a 'long complete' in *Woman's Own*.

I'm glad I'm going with Pandora. I like her very much, she's the only person I know who can sit in the ante-room, gnawing at great bones and cracking them for the marrow, grease running down her chin, and yet still remain to all intents and purposes a perfect English lady.

Wednesday, 7th

Having fixed ourselves up with night duty, the next problem was what to wear.

'Scarves are essential,' Pandora said, 'preferably silk ones with something horsy on them.'

Luckily she had two, and mine was completely covered with foxes' heads and riding crops. It went very well with my sporty tweed suit.

Hamish picked us up at the bus stop and we drove beside a gorgeous salmon river to a pink castle on a hill. Not a real mediaeval one, he said, just Victorian Scottish baronial.

As he swaggered into the ancestral hall, six foot odd of healthy manhood bursting out of his Norfolk jacket and plus-fours, two of the largest and blackest sporting dogs I've ever seen hurled themselves at us, paws planted firmly on our shoulders, their clamour making the chandeliers tremble.

With a casual 'Down Shamus! Down Hero!' Hamish led us into the huge drawing room dominated by a life-size crucifix. Catholicism is obviously very big with this family.

He seized an antiquated bell-rope and gave it a good tug.

'I don't know why I do this,' he said. 'Nothing ever happens.'

After another couple of pulls the rope came away in his hand so he went to fetch the whisky himself.

We were halfway through our first double when a ruddy face came round the door.

'Did yer ring, Hamish?' (All the servants appear to be on first name terms with the family.) Hamish said not to worry, he'd fetched it himself already.

'Guid,' said the aged retainer, 'I'll be awa to clean Shimi's buits then.'

Soon two more members of the house-party arrived from a morning's duck shooting. They both had huge, hairy plus-fours and bristling moustaches and said, 'Hah d'ye do!'

We talked about ducks for nearly a quarter of an hour, then, to an imaginary flourish of trumpets, in stalked Lord Lovat himself, not looking at all like a commando, in pin-striped trousers, green tweed jacket and an orange suede waistcoat.

Our first impression was that he was quite fiendishly good-looking. He has a terrific figure and carries himself well. But when you get close to him you notice he has rather small eyes and an inclination to put on flesh under the chin – not *quite* my *Daily Mirror* hero!

His wife is lovely and unaffected, she wears a filthy old tartan skirt and no make-up. Holding her by the hand was the 'young master', a fiercely beautiful boy of four with red cheeks and a lock of hair hanging over his nose, two inches of kilt and a silver dirk. He has a deep bass voice and walks slightly bow-legged.

Pandora and I had had no breakfast, and were dreadfully hungry, and the whisky was rapidly going to our heads. There was an unbearable hiatus before lunch during which our stomachs started to rumble and we had to talk brightly and loudly to cover it up.

Lunch was a bit tricky. Spaghetti (our first course) is awfully difficult to eat when your hand is shaking with nerves. Also I started off with the wrong fork and had to juggle around like mad to get things straightened out before the savoury, which completely spoilt my enjoyment of the venison stew. Pan, of course, is used to grand life and behaved with much more *savoir faire*.

After lunch Hamish, who had hitherto ignored me completely, said, 'You won't mind coming out with the shoot, will you? Nothing else to do around here, y'know!'

I wiped the sweat from my brow. How could I tell him I was totally gun-shy – that when a child I used to leave tea parties early for fear of the crackers?

But there was no escape. Rosie Lovat took me up to her bedroom and fitted me out with a pair of Shimi's khaki socks and her own size 7 brogues for squelching through bogs.

We piled into an aged car which had to be pushed down the hill to start, hissing and bubbling and sending out clouds of boiling steam. Every now and then they would chuck some water over it to prevent it blowing up.

For the first shoot I stood with Hamish behind a juniper bush on top of Eskdale Moor. The Beauly river winds through the valley below, the mountains were purple with heather and the sun shone from a clear blue sky, but I was far too petrified to enjoy the scenery.

Suddenly a pheasant shot up, whirling against the sun. With one pantherine movement Hamish's gun flew to his shoulder, my fingers flew to my ears and the bird wavered and dropped like a stone.

I squealed and jumped up and down with excitement because I'd been so frightfully brave, and the bang, after all, had been quite small. Hamish, of course, thought all the excitement was for his deadly prowess and muttered, 'Thank God I didn't miss!' As a matter of fact, nobody seemed to be missing anything – I've rarely seen such widespread and accurate slaughter.

We strolled down through the woods, Hamish bowling over a few defenceless rabbits *en passant*, me trailing behind with the cartridge bag. Soon we were met by the traditional dour ghillie with yet another of those fiendish black dogs.

Hamish immediately became quite alarmingly 'in character', being jovial yet masterly, and calling the awful dog 'a pretty bitch' to which the ghillie replied in gibberish.

73

'Ay, a bonnie bitch but nae gey guid fer brungin' oot book!'

What on earth was a 'book' I wondered – alas it turned out to be a buck, the prettiest little deer, which Lord Lovat shot, much to my dismay.

Meanwhile I was admiring Hamish, who was resting on his laurels, gun over shoulder with one foot planted on a granite crag. I gloated over the noble calf swelling out of his plus-fours, the stomach held well forward and the behind well out. He had one of those gorgeous, jutting, compact Highland bottoms that suit a kilt so well.

I had hoped that from time to time he might have thrown me a small word of intimacy, or even tenderness, but he remained as aloof as if we had just met, his mind totally absorbed by the chase. While I was wilting with admiration, he was obviously thinking what a dreadful little girl I was, calling a buck a doe, and putting my fingers in my ears shamelessly under the very noses of sneering ghillies.

He must have seen my dismal face because he finally put his arm around my shoulders and said, 'Don't worry, old gel, you did all right – apart, of course, from that time you got in front of the guns. I really thought you were going to get peppered in the backside when old Shimi fired at that low-flying snipe!'

Home we went in the rickety car, birds and buck in the dicky, and Pandora in the back with the dogs who smelt terrible.

I've never in my life been so glad to see a tea trolley spread before the fire, all laden with hot oatcakes and honey in the comb, and Shimi and Hamish fighting like kids over the last chocolate biscuit, and the smelly old gun dogs steaming in front of the fire. The aged retainer staggered in again and said, 'Hae ye done, Rosie?' (to Lady L) and staggered out with the trolley.

We said we had to leave in order to go on night duty, but first we were whisked upstairs for a final strange ceremony. Every castle has its secret and theirs was Uncle Maurice, who has *paralysis agitans* and is bedridden.

He was sitting up in bed, a strange little old man in striped pyjamas with a Catholic priest crouched at the end of the bed and a talking budgerigar sitting on his shoulder. He was shaking and could hardly speak, but I suddenly realised he was Maurice Baring whose writing I used to admire so much when I was at school. It really gave me quite a turn when I realised who he was. He let me hold the budgerigar who is called Dempsey.

We left, clutching dead pheasants, with hardly a chance to say goodbye to Hamish or thank him for such a fantastic day. I only hope he rings again!

Thursday, 8th

After two days of silence the phone finally rang, to my enormous relief. Would I like to come over and meet the dowager Lady Lovat and her daughter Veronica, who live in a little house on the estate? Would I like to shoot some teal?

Yes to the first, no to the second, so just in case, I went to the chemist and bought something called Quies, which are little pink balls of wax that you stick in your ears.

We had the usual whip-round for suitable clothes – Oscar's brown jersey, Pandora's tweed coat, and the horsy scarf.

Hamish picked me up at Brockies Corner and drove to Clunes where Veronica and the dowager were planting bulbs in the garden.

Laura, Lady Lovat, is quite amazing, straight from the Yellow Book period, a tall thin creature in black floating chiffon and gum boots. Her hands and feet are incredibly long and her hair is piled wildly on top of her head like Scotch mist. She has huge lovely eyes like a mad deer and amber-rimmed spectacles on the tip of her nose. She struck me as kind, cultured and witty, but most bizarre.

Her daughter Veronica is a pale edition of her, like a beautiful gazelle. There are two children, one and three, both angelic-looking. Veronica's husband is missing – no news of him for ages, and everyone is afraid he must be dead, but she is putting a very brave face on it, poor thing. There was also Ernesto, the Italian prisoner who 'works' in the garden. He was draped gracefully over his mattock, watching us with liquid brown eyes, a living monument to *dolce far niente*.

Nursery lunch was cold pigeon and prunes and custard and I drank a lot of cider to keep up my courage for the bangs to come.

We rattled off to a small loch where we sat on the bank and waited for the teal. They were sweeping over the water but rather far out, and Hamish suddenly began to make the most extraordinary noises, crooning and chirping in the back of his throat.

'What on earth are you doing?' I asked.

'Making teal noises,' he said gloomily. 'The buggers are all out of range.'

He couldn't have been a very convincing teal because the birds stayed right where they were, refusing to come and be killed – damned unsporting of them.

Then he spotted my ear plugs and laughed like hell. 'Gun-shy eh? Used to have a dog like that!'

'What did you do? Have it put down?'

'You seem to think I'm the most awful shit, but I'm not really.' He took my chin in his hands. 'You know, there's something very refreshing about you, Joanie, you're different – I like your squint, too, it's very sexy.' Isn't life wonderful!

It started to rain and we sheltered under some pines. He put his arm round me and I thought 'here it comes' – but no! Instead he started talking about religion and politics. Apparently he takes his Catholicism very seriously, and doesn't have any women at all, apart from whores and the occasional South American adventuress. A nice Catholic girl like me scares the pants off him. He has a very hearty expectation of his own damnation which I sympathise with a lot.– I have not met anyone recently – part from myself – who expects anything but eternal beatitude. But it doesn't make one's sex life any easier!

Much to my delight, we discover we are related through Percy Wyndham – so I'm a 'cousin', whatever that may mean. It seems a vague sort of term in the snob world meaning that you are 'all right'.

He's very keen on politics, having been president of the Oxford Union and so on, but I'm hopeless, and know nothing about such things at all. He told me about his ambitions which are to be a millionaire, a good poet or prime minister – preferably all three. 'Actually, money rather bores me,' he said, 'except for the idea of having a very great deal of it.'

Then the rain started to come down in earnest, so we went home for tea: honey and baps round a roaring fire. I think they are a very nice family, cheerful and lazy, and great scholars. All the farmers around seem to adore them.

It was one of the pleasantest afternoons I had spent for a long time, and as the bus arrived Hamish pressed into my hand a pair of silk stockings from Italy, fine and beautiful like cobwebs.

Sunday, 11th

Celebrated my twenty-first with Pandora, Oscar and Zoe Hicks, a very jolly new officer who is Augustus John's daughter. She has slanting gypsy eyes and does mad Hungarian dances at parties.

We made a wonderful rum punch and invited the rest of the Mess to join us. The punch was a killer – whisky, gin, rum, lemon squash and cucumber, all stirred up in a bucket.

Zoe did her famous dance and fell over, splitting her beautiful red dress right up the back.

To my delight and amazement Hamish had remembered the date and sent me a book of Donne's poems bound in green leather.

Wednesday, 14th

I am now showing alarming signs of being in love with Hamish. I feel sick, and my stomach doesn't like the idea of food which means that I really have got it badly.

His leave ends next week and he wants me to spend a few days with him at Eil-en-Aigus, which means the island in the middle of the Aigus. It's an amazing house belonging to Lady Lovat, sitting right in the middle of a rushing river.

'Well,' Oscar said, 'if he doesn't make a pass at you there he never will!'

Thursday, 15th

He picked me up at the bus stop and drove me to the island. Such a lovely house – lamplight and harpsichords with broken strings, and bunches of dried flowers hanging on the backs of bedroom doors.

Met by Lady Lovat looking very strange in wonderful pointed boots with criss-cross garters, a sheepskin coat and long dangling earrings of seed pearls. She was attended by a fierce-looking abbé in a flowing black cloak, who had come over from France to stay with her.

Chicken risotto for lunch and I ate nothing. As Hamish was commenting on my minuscule appetite, the butler bore in his favourite pudding, an enormous apple dumpling on a silver platter, which he devoured like a tiger, while my stomach shrank into ever smaller knots.

After lunch we all sang round the piano and Hamish performed his *chef d'oeuvre*, 'Water Boy', with a voice like a whizzed and tone-deaf bumble bee stuck in a bottle. I managed a quavering rendition of 'When I am Laid in Earth' from *Dido and Aeneas*, and then Lady L and I tore off a couple of Bach piano duets with great gusto and much wrestling for the middle clef.

After that everybody suddenly became terribly tactful. Veronica rushed off to do gardening, Lady Lovat lay down for a little rest, and the abbé, who is very athletic, changed into some rompers and rushed off to climb some rocks.

Hamish and I looked at one another in embarrassed silence. Finally he said, 'Shall I – er – drag you round the island?'

He put on an enormous grey Stetson hat which he calls his plantation hat. This made him look so alluring I practically fainted. For about an hour I was dragged through nettles, brambles, bogs and swarms of stinging flies. Every now and then he would fling himself flat on his stomach to stalk something. 'Look, a caper-cailzie!' or 'Look, gauzers!' Down I would have to go with him, ripping my new stockings.

At one point, lying nose-to-nose on the swampy ground, he gripped my arm and said, 'God, I want to rush madly to bed with you!'

I gazed ecstatically into his eyes, my mouth trembling for his kiss, but suddenly a big greeny-bronze thing like a turkey shot out of the bushes with the speed of a bullet.

'Capercailzie!' shouted Hamish triumphantly, dropping my arm and leaping to his feet. There is nothing like a game bird for taking a Scotsman's mind off romance. It wasn't until we were walking home for tea that he finally broached the subject again.

'I shall be going up to London for a couple of days when my course ends. Would you like to come with me?'

This, indeed, was it.

'But,' I stammered, 'I thought you didn't . . .'

'Didn't what?'

'Oh, you know, go with girls because of – er – the Catholic thing.'

Hamish looked gloomy, then his face brightened. 'Oh well, we'll just have to have a beautiful friendship, won't we? Or if by any chance things get out of hand we'll just have to go to Confession, eh?'

I sat down to tea glowing with happiness, my appetite miraculously returned, and I ate four baps and two slices of fruit cake.

The abbé was glowing, too, from his exertions. Apparently his cousin, who is *'presque* bishop', is incarcerated in a fortress and the abbé is practising to rescue him. After tea he sang French hunting songs and did animal impersonations. He made a very good cat, but Lady L drew the line at *le cochon*.

Hamish and I had no further opportunity to be alone. At one point Veronica drew me aside and hissed, 'How are you getting on?' So I guess she's on my side, which is nice because I like her a lot.

Next morning

I woke very early to a perfect morning, and looked out of the window. The whole island seemed as if it were on fire, smoking up to the rising sun. The mist rose from the river, up through the pine trees to the blue sky, and arranged itself into white clouds.

79

Every branch, leaf and needle glittered with dew and caught fire from the sun's rays.

Hamish popped his head round the door, commented rather rudely on the chasteness of my nightgown and said we were off to hear Mass in Aunt Sybil's private chapel at Maniock Castle. Life here, it seems, is just one terrifying incident after another.

Lots of hothouse flowers and candles, with aged retainers in black mantillas, one of which I was lent to wear over my head. The Lovats have their own private gallery – a sort of dress circle – and the whole family were there.

I was bowed in prayer, and on raising my head found Lord Lovat beside me in yellow waistcoat and corduroy trousers, which quite put me off my prayers and caused my empty stomach to rumble uncontrollably. I caught Hamish's reproving eye.

As we walked out into the sunshine he took my arm, laughing. 'Dancing bearies,' he said, 'that's what my nanny used to call it when your tummy rumbled.' So I suppose the whole chapel had heard!

Breakfast that followed was equally paralysing, as I was trapped between Lady Sybil and the priest, and my sausage – a burnt one – hopped off my plate and landed in my lap when I attempted to spear it. Everyone pretended not to notice – it was awful!

Back in time for the afternoon watch, which was rather soporific, just a few Hurricanes out of Wick and the odd Spitfire from Sumburgh. Over endless cups of tea we discussed the possibility of transferring to some other job – Ops, or Codes and Ciphers – anything to get to an operational station and see some action! But there's not much hope once you're stuck in Filter.

Hamish rings to say that he's off on his 'hush-hush' course soon, but will be in London for the odd weekend. Can we meet up? I'll have to wangle a crafty forty-eight hours.

Saturday, 31st

He's got his weekend and I've got my forty-eight, so rushed up to London and made for Nell Gwyn House. Ever since we were bombed out of Milborne Grove Mummy and Sidonie have been camping out there in a tiny one-room flat. Sid sleeps on a camp-bed in the bathroom. Most of the furniture is still over at the house, which wasn't badly hit, just made unsafe to live in. Considering how cramped they are they get on remarkably well, apart from the odd row over bathroom territory!

Hamish turned up in his best Savile Row suit, and my mother talked to him about silkworms and the war. I think they got on frightfully well. He is rather sad not to be still with his old unit in Africa. They are in the thick of it at Alamein. Apparently Hitler made a speech a couple of weeks ago saying that commandos landing in Europe and Africa will be slaughtered to the last man, which hasn't gone down too well with the Lovats!

Mum is in good spirits because there have been no bombs for several weeks. She mentioned at one point that she had got me a single room upstairs for my leave as there was obviously no room in her own flat – I could see that this point was not lost on Hamish.

I was wearing a wonderful black dress with padded shoulders and my cameo bracelet, with earrings to match. Off we went to the Bagatelle where the doorman mistook him for Shimi, much to his delight.

'Oh, but you're much better looking than Shimi,' I said.

'What, better looking than old Shimi? Why, I must be the best-looking man in the world then!'

Society tarts kept rushing up to him, giving me sidelong glances charged with venom. The place glittered. Everyone was very smart and there was an air of hysterical gaiety, quite intoxicating after Inverness. The prices were fantastic. There were two bands but no room to dance.

'There are only two thoughts in the heads of all these people,' H said, 'copulation and death. The first, of course, is perennial but the Luftwaffe seems to have given a lot of impetus to the latter.'

Three martinis later we were both floating.

'After the war,' declared Hamish, 'I will take you to Brazil, and we will create a new heaven and a new earth with our two bare hands, far from this decadent and dying civilisation.'

I lay on his shoulder drinking it all in, although I knew it was a lot of nonsense.

From there we went to the Gargoyle where we waltzed rather clumsily to the 'Blue Danube', and I didn't realise how drunk I was until I saw my hand in slow motion knock a glass of whisky to the floor. Happy as sandboys, we trucked around the slippery floor to the 'St Louis Blues'.

'If you don't like my peaches,' I sang into his ear, 'why do you shake my tree? Get out of my orchard and let a poor girl be.'

'Oh, but I do like them, Joanie, I like them very much indeed.'

I suppose it was about then that I realised I was going to have to go to bed with him.

We ended up at the 400 Club, the most pukka session yet. The bowing waiters, the private bottle of brandy. It was very dark with soft red lights and white flowers on a spotlit piano. In the distance was the jungle whisper of the band playing 'Brazil'. Hamish put his arm round me and my bones melted.

'You know, I really like taking you out, you're so different.'

Oh dear, not again!

'Yes you are, you're different from all the rest of my set. They really bore me to tears, but you're so stimulating and refreshing!'

I told him that line had whiskers on it but neither of us really cared. We were too happy. Apparently, apart from me, the only other girls he really likes are tarts.

'What's so great about them!' I asked.

'Well,' he explained, 'you know that you only have to see the silly girls once, so you can go to Confession the next day with a perfectly firm "purpose of amendment", whereas with someone like you, whom I'm rather fond of, I jolly well know I'll want to see you again.'

Needless to say, he doesn't want to get married. He's frightened of losing his freedom! Oh dear, oh dear, hang the flag at half-mast and play the Dead March from Saul! Really a gel starts to wonder. He says that if he ever does marry it will have to be a goddess. He could never brook the slightest imperfection in a wife. I began to feel more and more gloomy.

'But, of course, Joanie,' he went on, 'I could always groom you, make you smart and buy you fur coats. You know, you could be quite a beautiful person if you took a little trouble.'

Damned condescending bastard!

Well, the evening finally came to an end and we took a taxi to Nell Gwyn House. After a few minutes he took me in his arms and kissed me properly for the first time. It wasn't very nice because the taxi was very bumpy and our mouths kept getting unstuck.

'Do you really like me?' he asked at one point as the taxi lurched us apart.

'Of course, or I wouldn't be kissing you.'

'So I can come back to your room, can I?'

The crunch!

Well, I was drunk, weak and I could see no real reason for saying no. I think I must be a terrible snob because I seem to find it awfully difficult to say no to a member of the aristocracy – the thought of all that blue blood pounding in their temples reduces me to a quivering jelly. Also I knew he would leave me if I didn't.

We tiptoed upstairs and turned on the gas and he made me undress first. He said I had a figure like a Grecian urn.

Then he threw off his jacket and shirt and under it was this massive silver crucifix with a bit of some obscure saint's bones stuck in it. Down clanked the reliquary on to his spotless under-pants, and there he was, huge and tall, in the firelight. 'Je suis prest,' he announced – my family motto! 'Yes, so I see.'

'Whores usually think I have rather a good bodah!' he went on rather pompously as he warmed his bum in front of the fire. Then he lay down and I started kissing him. He seemed pleased and surprised that I was so affectionate, and kept calling me 'Sweetie'.

Then he started to make love to me. He was enormously heavy, and it was rather boring and seemed to go on for hours. I tried to remember what Jo had told me in Redcliffe Gardens about what men liked, and wriggled as much as I could – but it was difficult

83

under all that weight. I felt nothing, but I must have been convincing because he kept saying I was wonderful and terribly good in bed. I suppose if you usually have tarts anything seems nice. But the worst thing was that he found it awfully difficult to have an orgasm. Something kept happening to him just as he was getting to the point.

'What's the matter?' I finally asked in despair, thinking this was going on forever.

'It's that damned Confession business,' he muttered. 'Every time I'm just about to come I have a sort of flash of the Jesuits in Farm Street and Father Petrocelli looming out of the Confessional like a jack-in-a-box in his black cassock.'

'Never mind,' I said and, putting on my dressing-gown, I sat beside him stroking his hair and kissing him, and telling him it didn't matter. He's so sweet, so unbearably attractive. What a pity Catholicism has messed him up so.

He kissed me goodbye and said, 'When I am Emperor of Brazil you shall be my Empress.'

He would have liked to stay but he has to get up terribly early tomorrow to get to church before he catches the train back to his training camp. He still won't give me any hint as to what he's up to.

Sunday, 1st November

Mass at the Servites with Mum and Sid which was a bit of a nightmare as I couldn't take Communion, being in a state of mortal sin. I pretended it was because I had drunk some champagne by accident after midnight, but I don't think they believed me!

Later we heard on the wireless that Canterbury was badly bombed last night for the first time.

5th December 1942

Got quite a nice letter from H saying, 'I find you a rather difficult – in fact *very* difficult person to write to. You're immensely and pungently critical. Writing to you I feel I'm offering my dreary auto-erotic self to your eagle eye and claw upon a platter. Let that be – I'm yours for the rending – on paper!

'I want to thank you enormously for your company in Scotland and in London. I kept asking you then if you were bored. I wonder if you were. I certainly wasn't and I doubt if you were.'

How weird that he should even imagine such a thing when I was totally riveted with excitement the whole time!

We are now having a spell of beautiful frosty weather. The roofs and bridges look as if they are made of hard white sugar under a clear green-blue sky. All the dead leaves have frozen hard, and crackle like fire when we walk through them. Christmas is approaching and we are busy decorating the Mess.

25th December 1942

My first Christmas in Scotland. I had behaved so well for the last few months, and everyone here thought I was such a nice, quiet intellectual little girl – but not any more!

We were up at the men's Mess, and it was fantastic – colossal buffet, unlimited booze. I decided to break out and go on a jag. I can't remember when I got so drunk or felt so exhilarated, except possibly when I went out with my dad.

I have an awful feeling I called the CO a stinker – it was one of those religious arguments about whether the popes had mistresses.

602, our international squadron, flew over for the party and parked their Spitfires practically in our backyard.

I remember waltzing and eating plum pudding simultaneously, and then being sick in the laurels.

A very nice pongo drove me home and wanted to kiss me but I said No, and he said God, what a swine I am trying to take advantage of a gel when she's tight!

Mama wrote saying how much she had liked Hamish. Also sent me a kettle -- unobtainable up here -- some ginger nuts, some Persian oil, and a beautiful silk kimono. What's more she says she will pay for me to have a facial at Arden and Raymond when I come on leave. Apparently Monsieur Raymond is very smooth and soigné and wears sandals!

The dressing-gown has been a great success. The girls tell me I look the personification of sin in it. I wonder why? I suppose one connects kimonos with Brighton.

Petya's letter is very typical. He himself spent Christmas in a state of 'pale madness -- but still my bright image shone through a haze of tears, white against the blood of Stalingrad and the grey shadows of the Indian famine'! If only he would write me a normal, funny letter, just once, and stop striking poses.

Twelfth Night

This was our opportunity to show the men how it's done. We gave a wonderful Twelfth Night party with masks and forfeits and a Lord of Misrule. For days we had worked, making masks and scraping out turnips to make lanterns -- God, it was fun.

We danced like angels in darkened rooms lit only by lanterns. I was with a little Canadian pongo from Beauly, the world's most soul-satisfying dancer. I wore a very tasty black mask with curving gold wings, which went very well with my black and gold Russian cigarettes.

Finally exhausted, we flopped on a sofa in a lonely corner where he could talk to me about his soul -- his name is Ernest. We found we had much in common, including a liking for Pernod, Shakespeare and Thurber.

14th January 1943

A most unexpected letter arrived from Rupert. I was so taken aback I burst into tears! He says he was suddenly overcome with nostalgia for the good old days and thought perhaps we might be pen-pals and meet *sub rosa* for an occasional jolly lunch when on leave. I'm still awfully fond of old Rupert, strangely enough – I suppose one always is of one's first boyfriend.

He also gives me the amazing news that Gerhardt is alive and living in London! Apparently he was put on a different ship, not the *Arandora Star*, and has spent the war in an internment camp in Australia. Hearing he was alive gave me quite a shock as I remembered that snowy winter when I yearned for him so much, and we were all singing 'Over the Rainbow' and 'My Heart Belongs to Daddy'. I am much happier now but those tunes still bring it back to me, those extraordinary times, his studio in Cavaye Place, and all the feelings of misery and excitement that go with first love. It seems now like a world that never existed except in my own mind, but sometimes it comes back vividly, like the memory of a dream, making me shiver and sweat with remembered anguish and longing.

He is very anxious to meet me again so I think I'll organise a crafty forty-eight and go up and see him. Apparently he is working as an air-raid warden, and has a garret in Euston.

2nd February 1943

Took the night train, having arranged for Gerhardt to meet me on Euston Station.

At first sight he seemed to have changed very little – still that villainous, dramatic look, that cynical smile, the amber eyes mocking me. He was wearing his ARP dark blue greatcoat and beret, and old scuffed leather gloves which he took off to hold my cold hands. His corduroy pants, bleached by the Australian sun, are now practically silver, like birch trees.

He lives at the top of a squalid-looking house behind Euston

Station in a room known as 'Minnie's Garret'. It is kept by an ex-artist's model called Mrs Balasteros, who wears Spanish shawls and does her hair in a bun.

Inside there is scarcely any light – a ladder leading to a kind of platform with an iron bedstead on it and a cracked basin in the bathroom.

When we arrived Mrs B was in the kitchen bathing her six children, five by Mr B and one by a Portuguese who she had in an air-raid shelter. This one was sitting in the sink amongst the cabbages and saucepans and squinting violently. Another boy was under the table feeding a rabbit, and another was firing a toy pistol at his mother. This was Pedro on leave from his reform school.

We went up to the top floor and Gerhardt took off his overcoat and beret. I noticed then that he was very thin and his hair was receding slightly – he really looked as if he had 'been through it'. He had a hard time in a British concentration camp in Australia and said that for cruelty the Germans have nothing on the Aussies!

He seemed in a high state of jitters, swallowing Luminal pills from a little turquoise box to slow down the action of his heart, and coughing consumptively. He says he keeps a Philippine sword by his bed with which to kill himself if the Germans come. I asked him if he still played his flute but he said no, it was pinched by soldiers on board HMS *Dumera*.

I found myself looking hard at his face, trying to find any trace of the man I loved so desperately only a few years ago, the one who gave me my very first kiss. But now that I'm with him and seeing him again I feel nothing. It's very strange. After Hamish, so normal and clean, he seems old and rather grubby. I used to think of him as the Great God Pan – now he seems more like a goat!

Anyway, there I was, and I thought I'd better make the best of it, so I cut up garlic for the fish pilau and played with his Siamese kitten who was after the squid.

After lunch he drew me to my feet and kissed me with his pointed snake-like tongue. I felt my body stiffen as he pressed closer to me, kissing my neck and saying how much he liked the smell of my hair.

'Well, Joanie, shall we go up to bed?' He looked up the ship's ladder towards the rumpled unmade bed on the platform. By now I was so nervous that I began to laugh.

'No, no, you mustn't laugh – there is a certain ceremony about these things. And anyway, it's bloody uncomfortable down here.'

I took a deep breath and said, 'I'm terribly sorry, Gerhardt, I can't do it.'

Gerhardt put on his fake Hollywood accent.

'Whatsa matter, don't ya love me any more?' He had a sudden thought. 'Jesus Christ, you're not still a bloody virgin, are you?'

'No, of course I'm not!'

I decided to exaggerate the Hamish episode a bit so as not to make him feel too bad. 'The fact is I'm madly in love with this Scottish boy and I just find I can't do it with anyone else, that's all. I did think about it on the train,' I went on, 'because I thought that perhaps I could – but I find I can't and that's it, and I'm really very sorry.'

Gerhardt regarded me with cold speculation. 'Well, well. You're a hard little bitch nowadays, aren't you?'

'Maybe I am,' I said. 'It's better than being a stupid one.'

'I think I liked you better when you were stupid – a stupid little virgin and madly in love with me.'

I was beginning to feel pretty embarrassed, also rather disgusted with my own behaviour, when luckily the tension was broken by a loud scream and a string of Spanish oaths from the garden below. Mrs Balasteros had put all her bedding out to dry on the lawn, and a Frenchman had peed on it from the second floor window. We roared with laughter and suddenly everything was all right again.

After it was dark we went for a pub crawl in Chelsea and Soho with a view to cadging drinks, food and money from Gerhardt's friends who frequent them. We went to the Nelson, the Cadogan, the Studio Club, the Swiss, the York Minster, and the Café Bleu. Gerhardt lives, he tells me, entirely on his wits, going on these 'diurnal excursions of a predatory nature' and occasionally managing to cadge dinner invites from old friends who have coronets on their napkins. The only money he has left is concentration camp money, specially designed by the inmates with a pattern of barbed wire and sheep, and sexual insults cleverly intertwined among them, so you can only read them with a magnifying glass.

It was nice being with him. Every now and then we would look at each other and exchange a smile of complete understanding. He says he is glad I am happy and only wishes he had made more of his opportunities when I was seventeen!

We ended up at the Café Royal, where he talked for about two hours about himself, his work, his women, his fearful privations and the fact that there is something wrong with his brain.

By now I had had enough, so I told him that I was very tired and we went back to Mrs Balasteros who was sitting in front of a bowl of horrible entrails singing flamenco. She gave me a squalid room for two shillings a night, and the following morning I went back to Inverness.

Gerhardt and I parted warmly enough, but made no plans to see each other again. I think he is a nice old bastard, rather pathetic really, and quite sensitive under that cynical veneer, but I could never, never love him again.

14th February 1943

St Valentine's Day

Pandora and I were at a very boring dance at the Caledonian Hotel, complete with exhibition of Highland dancing. The Cally, as everyone calls it, is the social centre of life round here. Just before the last waltz a very smooth pongo dragged us off to a party at the Cameron Barracks. The Mess had been turned into the Moulin Rouge. There was a swing pianist, and lots of jolly officers dancing on top of the bar with the local tarts and the waitresses from the Cally.

Two hefty sergeants did the can-can, throwing their legs in the air to show their frilly knickers.

I took a little Benzedrine (pinched from my dad) and remained completely sober in spite of gin, crème de menthe, rum and

Algerian wine, which was just as well as I was locked out and had to climb over a ten-foot spiked gate.

Dirty looks from Gloves, who spotted me.

Saturday, 13th March

The Canadians held a prize fight in a field for Salute the Soldier Week, and Ernest invited me.

The British Empire champion fought a quite fascinating negro with long, concave, golden thighs. Lots of blood. Then back to the Mess to shoot rats in the pig stys and eat tinned corn and tinned peaches. Ernest gave me some clothing coupons.

Life has settled into a fairly boring routine, and spring seems a long way off. 'Don't worry,' Oscar said, 'the Norwegians will be back soon. I've had a letter from Danny, the maddest one of all, and their boat will be in for a refit by the end of April.'

Refits always take a good few weeks, what with re-painting, checking the guns and torpedoes, and overhauling the engines, so now we have something to look forward to.

Friday, 30th April

I first met the Norwegians in the Cally bar, where everything happens.

I was sipping my gin and lime when a voice behind me said, 'Has anyone ever told you you look like Ingrid Bergman?' I was about to crush the intruder with 'Oh dear, not that corny old line again!' when I saw it was a Norwegian – and what a Norwegian! He was six feet tall with soft floppy blond hair, blue eyes – large and very deeply set – and the face of an angel. He was immaculate in his dark blue uniform of a first lieutenant in the Norwegian Navy.

'Hans Gundersen,' he said, holding out his hand, 'and that's my Captain Danny over there, the boldest man in the Norwegian Navy.'

'If you mean the one on all fours who is barking like a dog, I think you should stop him before he bites the barmaid in the leg.'

'Ah – excuse please!'

He returned with a small monkey-faced man, obviously whizzed as a newt, walking as if he had springs in his feet. His hair was tow-coloured and his eyes Mongolian. He was wearing the DFC and bar. With him came Otto, their navigator, a suave character with hooded eyes – town man to Hans's country boy.

According to Otto, Danny is a living legend – on land he's like a crazy child, always drunk (he once jumped from a top floor window hanging on to an umbrella). At sea, he's the toughest captain in the whole flotilla, and goes into action in his pyjamas with a whaling knife clutched between his teeth.

Anyway, he seemed a pleasant enough chap, if a bit mad, and before I knew what I was doing, I had invited the whole flotilla to our May Day party in the Mess tomorrow.

Some of them have curious names like characters in a Norse Saga: Fir-tree-eater, Tie-eater, Chamber-pot-breaker and so on. On moonlit nights they sneak out from the Shetlands to the occupied Norwegian coast and lie in wait among the islands for the German ships to come past. Their boats have two torpedoes and a speed of thirty knots – tiny and frail, but they can out-manoeuvre bigger ships.

Now, for a couple of months, they are in dry dock at Thornbush for repairs and refitting.

Saturday, 1st May

Our Mess is very small so we are turning the back lawn into a beer garden with tables and music. The whole house is decorated with lilac.

I am on watch now counting the hours to 8 p.m. when our taxi comes and we can hare down to the Windsor to get our glamour on before the guests arrive.

9 p.m.

I had decided to wear my new dusky pink crêpe dress, £2 13s. from Miss Mackay's and worth every penny of it.

Pandora was in something floral, Oscar was in black, and we made a grand entrance together down the big central staircase.

The buffet and drinks were in the hall, the gramophone in the ante-room with the carpet rolled back for dancing.

We heard the Norwegians coming from a long way off, playing their national anthem on paper combs. In front marched Danny, carrying aloft the ship's mascot, a huge curly-horned sheep's head called George. He seemed like some tribal chief with his barbaric idol. Behind marched the flotilla. As they approached the Mess, they pocketed the combs, threw away the Jeyes paper and burst into the MTB flotilla song.

'Far out in the North Sea the little ships are lurking,' they bellowed.

Danny entered the Mess, bowed to the astonished 'Gloves', and deposited George on the bar.

'MTB 718, Captain Per Danielsen, reporting for duty, ma'am.'

He snapped his fingers and Hans started unloading six bottles of Aquavit from a paper bag.

'And now, we drink!'

The rest of the evening passed like a dream. Dancing is the thing I like best in life, and Hans proved to be a wizard dancer – we were first on the floor and the last to leave it. I danced with a narcissus between my teeth, and I can remember thinking – in the middle of a rumba – that I was so happy that I wanted to cry. I drank and drank and became beautifully merry, but at the same time my mind remained clear.

Later, we fell upon the buffet – lobster, salmon, mushrooms, asparagus, crabs, tinned peaches and ice-cream.

'And to think,' Hans said in amazement, 'that in Norway people are starving!' and then proceeded to tuck in like crazy.

After supper we wandered out into the garden and sat under the trees. I was on Hans's knee, and Oscar on Danny's, all of us drinking Aquavit. They taught us to sing the flotilla song, 'I – mellem holmer, i – mellem boer og skjaer,' which means, 'Through the little islands and through the little star shells.'

Hans's face in the moonlight was very beautiful. His complexion is so delicate, like porcelain, and when he blushes his ears go pink.

About 2 a.m. he and I wandered down the road to the Islands. It was a fine, warm night with a May moon, and we found a little puppet theatre among the trees where they do Punch and Judy in the summer. It had a tattered backcloth of lilacs, and we lay on the dusty sacking listening to the rushing water and watching the moon reflected in the river.

We kissed passionately for a long time, and I think maybe he would have gone further, but I didn't let him.

As we walked back home in the growing light, he said, rather to my amazement, 'I'm so glad you didn't let me have you, I would never have respected you if you had given in the first time!' Obviously these Norwegians are very unusual fellows, very strange and wonderful creatures.

Got home to find a dead drunk squadron leader in my bed, so slept on the sofa.

Next morning

Rose's lime juice – and yet more Rose's lime juice!

Friday, 7th May

Hans and I are seeing each other every day and I'm getting more and more fond of him. Danny is also dating Oscar, but not, I think, so seriously. The crew of 718 have a little attic at the top of a squalid boarding house called 'The Albert', which is full of stuffed owls and smells of cheese. Attached to it is a fierce rug-like dog who attacks all Sassenachs on sight.

Saturday

Today the heatwave started, and we took our lovers across the sea to Black Isle to lie in the sun. Saw wild geese flying and picked lilac.

I'm as brown as a berry. Life is a dream of spring and fine weather, moonlit nights and beautiful young men. We have, perhaps, three weeks still to go, then the boat leaves on operations again, leaving behind a trail of broken dolls.

In the meantime, there is our Wings for Victory week, which starts tomorrow, and should be great fun.

Six days later

Well, WFV week is finally over, and I have to report that the Norwegians (and in particular Danny) put up a pretty poor show – as follows.

Sunday: Hans and Danny get drunk at midday in the Station Hotel, and hang all the chamber pots out of the bedroom windows on long pieces of string, just as the Boy Scouts are due to start their Victory march past. Our boys then climb on to the façade over the railway station and start moving the hands of the clock back. Scouts in profusion, police called, Hans and Danny banned from the Station Hotel.

Monday: Dance at the Cally. Danny turns up with his old pal, the hotel Boiler Man, plus the youngest whale killer in Norway, a very tough and oily individual who insists on taking his trousers off and dancing on the table. Danny banned from Cally Hotel.

Thursday: Danny knocks three policemen unconscious and is hauled before the magistrate and fined £17. 'Make it £25,' says Danny, 'and the rest for the Spitfires!' Loud cheers from crew in the gallery.

My reputation is beginning to suffer, as my name is now irrevocably linked with the delinquent Norsks. On Friday Hans and Danny broke into the WAAF Mess roaring drunk (fresh supplies of booze having come on board) and stuck up the sergeant and orderlies with a Colt revolver. They demanded I should be brought down instantly, but thank God I was on duty.

Next day they turned up in the most frightful civvies – Homburg hats, check jackets, yellow boots and pearl tie-pins, hoping not to be recognised by the staff.

'We are incognito,' they hissed as I came down the stairs. 'Do we look like English gentlemen?' I said they looked like cads and bounders, but they insisted on taking me to dinner at the Station where Danny ate a whole bowl of red tulips with pepper and salt.

Well, I have now definitely had it with all this bad behaviour. I am sick and tired of it and wish they would grow up. Thank God Wings for Victory week is over.

All my airwomen, on the other hand, think Danny and Hans are absolute poppets. There is a great deal of mateyness and *lèse majesté* now that they've seen me dancing in civvies. Last night an ACW plonk congratulated me on my toenails and asked if she could call me Joan! Shockin' bad for discipline, what?

Meanwhile the heatwave continues, day after day of unbroken, cloudless sunshine, and lots of activity at work. Every 'drome in the area seems to be taking advantage of the fine weather to send up training flights.

17th May

Norwegian Independence Day. Great celebrations! We called early on the Norsks with huge bunches of flowers and found Danny still unconscious in bed embracing his stuffed sheep's head. We made them gallons of black coffee and sobered them up, while I washed George's curls with Amami shampoo in honour of the great day.

As soon as Hans was washed and shaved, I dragged him off to climb a little mountain called Dunain. He was wearing a white shirt and flannels, and looked like an illustration from *Woman's Own*. 'Ron smiled lazily down at Delia, his white teeth flashing against his tan,' etc.

We found a hollow that faced the sun and sank into a cushion of moss, looking out over the firth to the mountains beyond. We took off most of our clothes, ate tomato sandwiches and licorice allsorts, and drank beer.

'Tell me, what would a typical Sunday in Norway be like?' I asked lazily.

'Well,' said Hans, 'if it were winter you would open the window and see blue sky – then mother gives you dark bread and an orange for your knapsack, and you go into the woods on skis. The trees are hung with snow, and you lean your skis against a tree trunk and eat your bread, then you ski till three o'clock. Mother has the meat ready in a slow oven. You have sauna and then you eat like a king. First the roast beef, then '*multe*' with sour cream – little yellow berries that grow very high up where the ground is wet.'

I was beginning to think it all sounded rather idyllic and pictured myself meeting his mother – 'This is my fiancée, Joan Wyndham' – but then he started to describe the typical Norwegian girl, and any hopes I might have had of becoming Fru Gundersen faded rapidly. Apparently she treks for hours over the mountains in spring, swims, sails, and rows all summer, and skis from nine in the morning till nine at night in winter. Also, she never wears glasses. My glasses are a sore point with Hans. 'Pikener med brillene, fy faen!' he exclaims. 'Fy faen' is the worst thing any Norwegian can say, although it only means go to the devil! Hans says that in Norway only swotting students and old aunties wear glasses, not the sort of bronzed Valkyries he is used to going out with, so I spend most of my time taking off my glasses and bumping into things. Thank goodness my contact lenses will be ready in another three weeks or so.

Back in the Mess about six to get ready for tonight's ball at the Cally. Oscar admits that she is fascinated by Danny and I tell her I think I'm in love with Hans. When we got to the hotel we found a rather odd scene, Danny having invited some of his peculiar friends to join him – two porters from the station, the Cally doorman, the bouncer, two policemen and the filthy, pitch-black old man who keeps the hotel boilers stoked. He and Danny had already exchanged hats.

As the Cally is rather posh we were therefore relegated to a small room leading off the ballroom, where we sat with a bottle of whisky under the table, and two black soldiers from Honduras who had brought their ukuleles and played wizard jazz for us.

Everybody sang like hell, and by the time we'd got to the flotilla song, Hans, his arm around my neck, was shooting his famous death or glory line. Danny and Otto tend to become surrealistic when they are drunk but Hans only thinks about death.

Otto gave him his world-weary smile and said, 'But of course you will die young, my dear Hansemann, you haven't the face to make forty. Besides I've seen your life line – it stops in the middle.'

This was altogether too much for poor Hans who pulled me by the hand into the ballroom which was full of whooping Scotsmen in kilts doing eightsome reels. He dragged me into the centre of a circle and soon we were hopping like fleas to the obvious amazement of the kilted gentlemen.

When it came to the last slow waltz we whirled round and round the great ballroom without stopping, as if we were floating on air. I felt I was back in Old Vienna with chandeliers and violins playing.

When we returned to the little room, Danny had gone off to stoke the boilers with his friend and Otto had decided to catch a midnight train to London, so we walked to the Islands and stayed there till 2 a.m., playing Tarzan, climbing trees and wading in the icy river.

Hard-boiled eggs in bed.

Next morning

I definitely love him. It is the general opinion of my mates that if I don't stop whistling the Norwegian National Anthem half a note flat at all hours of the day or night there will be bloody murder done.

Yet only a few months ago I thought I was in love with Hamish. There is definitely something wrong with me – you're not supposed to be in love with two people at the same time.

I am worried that I may be one of those women who just take

on the colours of whoever they're with – perhaps there is no real me?

If only some all-possessing love would come along to redeem me – but I suppose it's a matter of what's in you, what you're capable of, what you can give. Perhaps I'm incapable of real love, and only take men from boredom, sensuality or vanity. Petya certainly thought so – 'smoking, drinking and copulation' he used to say, 'with you, these are just social gestures.'

So there you are – I think I love Hamish, I think I love Hans and I'd quite happily marry either one of them if they asked me!

Friday, 21st May

Hans has begun to show signs of mounting frustration. Much as he would like to respect me as a nice girl, I rather suspect that what he really wants is to sleep with me – but how difficult it is to find somewhere where we can make love!

We are tired of wandering late at night in the Islands or by the canal, lying on wet grass, kissing in church porches. Why do we have to drive each other mad like this? Hans hates snatching love in dark corners as much as I do, and I can see he is nearly going crazy.

Then Oscar told me about Drumnadrochit, an old hotel by Loch Ness where everybody goes for their dirty weekends. I mentioned it to Hans, saying we could get a twenty-four-hour pass and go there on our bicycles, and his ears went bright pink with pleasure.

'It's thirty shillings a night,' I warned him.

'Jeg har penge,' he said proudly, flashing a bulky wallet.

So we packed two small bags and set off on our bicycles for Loch Ness and Drumnadrochit. We had decided to make a day of it and go sailing first, visiting the Norwegian fishing boats moored on Loch Ness.

'We'll take the *Nancy-Elise*,' he said. 'She's moored on the far side of the loch. You will really like those Norwegian chaps, whale killers, seal hunters – the Captain Erling is my very good friend.'

'Yes, but first we must book into the hotel – do you think they'll ask for a marriage certificate?'

We needn't have worried. It is run by a couple of old dears with white whiskers who have refused to get married for fifty years and are living in sin at the age of ninety-three. They gave us knowing smiles as we signed in as Mr and Mrs Gundersen.

By now there was a lively gale blowing but Hans still insisted on taking out the *Nancy-Elise*. Reluctantly I let him row me across the loch.

We could hear the sound of an accordion coming across the water and much stamping of sea boots as we approached a boat called the *Medina*. The crew seemed to be doing a kind of wild rustic dance on board, while an old gnarled man played the squeeze-box.

We climbed down to the cabin where Erling sat in a green singlet and trilby hat, eating bacon off the end of his knife, and smelling strongly of fish. He was delighted to see us and directed us to a fourteen-foot boat, her scarlet sails flapping in the wind. I was already nervous as hell.

'Don't worry,' Hans said, 'I've been sailing since I was four.'

'Who's worried?'

'OK, then, start baling out while I rig her up.'

So off we went and were spanking towards the middle of Loch Ness, when there was a sharp crack and the rudder pin broke. Hans swore fiercely and tried to push it back – meanwhile we had no steering at all. A mighty gust took us broadside on and the boat keeled over and began to sink.

'Jump clear,' Hans shouted and I leapt into the icy water, bottomless, and full of treacherous currents. My trousers were very heavy and kept pulling me down.

I could see the boat floating keel side up some way away from me and struggled towards it. As I hung on to the bottom I saw an amazing sight. The gallant Hans, far from trying to rescue me, was only interested in keeping his wristwatch out of the water. He looked so damn funny, thrashing around with one arm and holding the other in the air, cursing and blaspheming at the same time, that I couldn't help laughing. This only added to his dreadful humiliation!

We were saved by Erling in his row-boat, who took us to the cabin, stoked up the fire, gave us whisky and hung up our clothes to dry. I was put into an old red jersey that stank of fish and some enormous trousers – every time I stood up the trousers fell down. We sang and ate bread and cheese very cheerily.

Hans and the boys then went off to salvage the *Nancy-Elise*, and I was left alone with Erling and the old accordion player who was now making a wooden boat for his grandson. After a while he yawned, put away his tools, and went creaking up the ladder.

In the light of a smoking oil lamp Erling fixed me with a meaningful look.

'You are nice girl. Very brave. And I like you. Maybe I give you a little kiss.'

I was rooted to the bunk, my trousers only held up by will-power. Erling lurched towards me through the gloom, the ancient and fish-like smell growing stronger by the minute. Desperately I ran for the ladder but my trousers fell down and I tripped and fell flat on my face at the foot of the stairs.

It was at this moment that Hans and the boys chose to arrive back, and I've never in my life pulled anything up so fast as those bloody trousers.

Luckily Hans didn't seem to notice anything. We drank final toasts, and Erling, frustrated in his evil intentions, departed in a huff by row-boat for a nearby farm where a lady (ambiguously referred to as his 'second cousin') was waiting for him. He put a large piece of cheese in his pocket to keep the dog quiet.

When we got back to the hotel I washed Hans's hair for him and we couldn't do anything with it, it was so shiny and soft, flopping over his eyes. We made love immediately, not waiting for night. I kissed him all over and called him my 'lille gul ungen min' – my little golden child.

He was so shy and inexperienced – I don't think he's had many girls before – and not really a very exciting lover, but I didn't mind because he was so sweet and handsome.

Later he lay back exhausted on the starched linen sheets, like a marble statue with a head of clay: his body white but his face and neck deeply tanned.

I hugged him all night, and in the morning I kept getting up and pretending to go to the bathroom, so that I could slip back into bed and accidentally wake him up and make love to him again. I was hoping that if we did it enough times something would happen – but it didn't. It was the same as always – I felt nothing, except for love.

He has only one hair on his chest and we looked for it in the morning to make sure it was still there and hadn't been rubbed off in the night.

Delicious porridge for breakfast. Then we found a little row-boat among a bed of reeds and as the owner was agreeable we rowed across the loch and landed at the ruins of Castle Urquhart – a most romantic ruin standing on a grassy promontory at the water's edge.

We explored the dungeons and then made love again amid the ruins, lying on the soft grass in the hot sun with our toes paddling among the yellow irises. That was the first time he ever said 'Jeg elske deg' which means 'I love you'. He also said that he would like to have babies with me, but I don't suppose he meant it.

We rowed back as the sun set. The loch seems immense when you are in the middle of it, huge as the Pacific Ocean, the mountains around turning pink. Incredibly beautiful! Hans said it was the happiest day of his life.

Monday

We swooped back to town on our bikes, a long gentle slope all the way, freewheeling for miles like the Big Dipper at Blackpool. A fresh breeze cooled our faces and we sang vulgar songs as we went. Hans knew a splendid one called 'The Man Who Had No Balls At All', which starts 'The night of the wedding I hopped into bed'. And then there was another which ends:

> Then gather round ye maidens
> And take advice from me
> Never trust a sailor
> An inch above your knee.

Well, I am now quite fantastically in love with him and realise I was never really in love before. He is, I imagine, like Adam must have been before the Fall, incapable of doing a mean or underhand thing. He has this untouched innocence about him that nothing seems to affect. How odd that one so handsome should also be so good!

I also like his sense of humour and his almost feminine sensitivity towards other men – I mean, of course, his companions-in-arms. 'Bloody pansies' make his blood boil!

Tuesday, 1st June

I had written to Dr Thomas saying I wanted to lose weight and he has sent me a prescription for one hundred Benzedrine – wonderful, just in time for my leave with Hans! He, Danny, Oscar and I plan to take London by storm on 6th June.

Meantime I have been given a super new job – Messing Officer. This means I'm in charge of the booze cupboard, and can order make-up for my friends. A big list went out today – two Cutex Cameo nail varnish, one Max Factor Pancake Natural No. 2, three refill Cyclax Velvet Grape lipsticks, two Coty Paris perfumes, and one Helena Rubenstein Apple Blossom perfume. I am now one of the most popular girls in the Mess. The only snag is I have to keep accounts.

I've also been given another job, not so nice, being Duty Officer at the WAAFs' hostel once a week.

Last night I was on duty when my NCO, who is a fearful busybody, reported that the sergeant (WAAF) of the hostel was sleeping with a blonde job from Ops. What was I going to do about it? Naturally I didn't want to do anything, especially as I know this sergeant, and she is very big and tough with an Eton crop. However, I had to report them, and the wretched girl will probably be posted.

Half an hour later one of the kitchen boilers blew up, and blew up an orderly with it. I am a nervous wreck.

Sunday, 6th June

ON LEAVE AT LAST

The moment when I stood at the window holding Hans's hand with the wind blowing against my cheek and the station moving away into the distance was one of the happiest moments of my life.

Danny was already in the carriage with Oscar, pouring Norwegian punch and whisky into a beer bottle and shaking them up. Needless to say they got very drunk. Danny, who has a very curious attitude to money, started tearing up £5 notes and throwing them out of the window.

Soon we were joined by a Norwegian pongo who had recently escaped from Norway and the Gestapo. We exchanged clothes and sang. Then the men passed out on top of us, Hans's head in my lap, Danny holding my hand, and the pongo on top of Oscar. This was very uncomfortable.

Hans has brought his Colt with him and threatens to shoot every bloody artist he meets on the off chance that they've been my lovers.

'I'll clean up Chelsea!' he mutters grimly.

What he would make of Rupert, Annie and the rest I shudder to think – as for a meeting between him and Petya, it would be epic.

At Euston they staggered out to a Turkish bath, feeling dreadful, while I went home to my mum's flat to wash and change.

Dinner at the Bristol Grill, where we did Apache dances. Then to tease Hans, I took him for a nightcap to the infamous Coffee 'An, where he sat among the pimps and pansies like some newly scrubbed angel.

'Who's that fuckin' public schoolboy?' I heard one tart mutter to another.

Slept at Nell Gwyn House. It was our third night together, and Hans cut notches on the bedpost with his commando knife in witness of his prowess!

Monday, 7th June

A wonderful hot day, so we went to Battersea Park and sat by the goldfish pond in the English Garden. We fed the birds and drank cider in a pub, all the typically English things which I hoped would impress Hans, and he picked white flowers for me to wear in my hair at the Embassy that night.

Dinner at Scott's, lobsters, strawberries and crêpes suzette. I just couldn't wait to go dancing, I felt as if I had ginger in my heels.

Arrived at the Embassy Club and Hans was thrilled because the head waiter recognised him, and I fell in love with a wizard nigger pianist and was delighted when he smiled at me.

We drank whisky and took Benzedrine and our legs felt as if they had springs in them. Neither Hans nor I had ever enjoyed a night out so much. Mario Barretti was playing Cuban music on drums and reed pipes, and I swayed in his arms to 'Brazil' and 'Black Magic'.

When we were exhausted I lay back on his shoulder watching the nigger's flying fingers playing a jazz version of Tchaikovsky's Piano Concerto No. 1.

At four in the morning, a sudden and harsh transformation took place. Bright lights went up, and the tables and chairs were stacked – a lonely waiter threw covers over the piano and drums. Suddenly everything was strange and garish in the white glare of the electricity. Our faces were tired and strained, and the white flowers in my hair were crumpled and dead. We looked at each other and laughed, then went home to bed.

Tuesday, 8th June

Iced rum punch at the Captain's Cabin with lots of Norwegian sailors, then the front row of the stalls for *The Merry Widow*. Oscar and I were dressed to kill in our black dresses with red roses in our hair. One of the chorus girls ogled Hans and his ears got very pink.

Our last night was very sad. We lay awake all night drinking whisky and talking about death. I cried and cried and he said, 'Don't cry, Jonnka, you know I'll come back for you.'

But at that time I was sure he would get killed – being on Danny's boat – and so was he. Even so, I'm glad he's not in bombers, or a fighter pilot – their life expectancy is even shorter, I'm sure.

Next morning our boys went back to Scotland, and Oscar and I, who had two more days, made tea and compared notes. I asked her how she had got on with Danny.

'Well, it's difficult to say really. He was so drunk every night that he never even got upstairs, let alone into bed! So I never had a chance to find out.'

'Well, I certainly did, and I don't know whether it's Hans's fault or mine, but I don't feel a thing. Of course, I just love being in bed with him and kissing him, but apart from that nothing happens.'

'I know a doctor,' Oscar said, 'a friend of mine went to him who had the same problem as us, and it seems we've got a thing called a clitoris, which makes us have an orgasm.'

'Yes,' I said, 'I've heard about that before.'

'Well, Dr Schliemann says they're very often not big enough, and he gives you some kind of ointment to make them grow.'

This thought so inspired us that we looked up Dr S in the phone book, and made an appointment to see him that very afternoon.

The consulting room was rather depressing, with a faint smell of antiseptic. A greenish light filtered through the blinds on to the huge mahogany desk. It was like being in an aquarium. A small, balding chap with glasses came in and said cheerily, 'Well, who's the first victim?'

Oscar went to sit in the waiting room, and I was laid out on a couch and examined in a most embarrassing way.

'Aha!' said Dr Schliemann, peering through his bifocals, 'I see you haven't got a man in your boat!' He sounded rather pleased at this discovery.

Then he went on to explain about the clitoris being a kind of magic trigger, but not to worry if I hadn't got one because he would give me a special cream to rub on every night. It costs thirty bob, and in no time at all he guarantees that I will have a clitoris 'long enough and strong enough to hang a copper kettle on'!

I duly forked out the thirty bob and received a small silver tube with printed instructions on it.

Later Oscar and I compared notes and found he'd said much the same thing to her except that he had asked her what sort of bed she slept on, and whether it was hard or not.

'Jewish people,' he had said, ' – or so I understand – do it on the floor.'

Oscar had got terrible giggles, trying to explain that in the WAAF you usually do it on the grass anyway.

We can't wait to try the magic ointment!

After leaving the doctor I found myself very near Cavendish Square, so decided to drop in and have another fitting for my contact lenses.

After half an hour of painful manoeuvring, the huge glass bubbles were finally in place, and I was sent off to take a walk around Oxford Street to see how they felt. I caught an amazing glimpse of my face in the windows of Debenhams and realised I had never really seen it before. A total stranger with wild, staring eyes, a crooked mouth and rather good cheekbones looked back at me. By now the lenses were beginning to hurt like hell, so I stumbled back to Cavendish Square and told them I thought they needed a bit more adjusting.

13th June

INVERNESS

Hans and I took a picnic to Black Isle, crossing the Moray Firth on the ferry.

The colours on the island were amazingly vivid – bright pinks, greens and yellows, with a kind of blue haze from the sea over everything. The grass was soft as a pile carpet that sinks beneath your feet, and the sea knocks in the rocks as if someone were following you.

There were rowan trees, honeysuckle and wild roses growing down to the water's edge, and black rocks splashed with orange lichen. Among the rocks we found a tiny field where a single tree sheltered a flock of golden sheep, their wool dyed the colour of honey. At first I thought they were stooks of corn until I saw their pink transparent ears.

We lay in an oasis of close-cropped grass, kept smooth by rabbits, and devoured wild raspberries. The sun warmed our faces, but everything around was unnaturally cool, fresh and green, as if it were still spring. There were little mounds of heather, and lime-green bilberries, the berries just starting to show their purple bloom. Every moss, sundew and star-shaped flower was perfectly formed – tiny, but fresh and full of sap. We lay in heavenly peace, just holding hands until nine o'clock. Then home for supper.

'And now for the fish and chips!' Hans always says. 'To feed certain bloody awful snakes I think you have in your stomach!'

It was very quiet on watch that night so I wrote a poem about Black Isle which went like this:

The sea had sung the field to sleep
And cradled it within a rock
And what I took for stooks of wheat
Were golden sheep in feeding flock.

The little field was all their world
Wherein they lay in timeless peace
And under one maternal tree
Rested their heavy ochre fleece.

The hollow stalks and nestling leaves
Were crucibles of light and dew
As if the mist and circling sea
Together kept them fresh and new.

As though the autumn and the spring
Had joined their hands in amity
To nourish with perennial food
The wild rose and the rowan trees.

The cool transparent breathing leaves
Were green as when they first unfurled
The scarlet berries never fell
As if a hand had stopped the world.

I showed it to Oscar, and she said it wasn't bad, but a bit '"school magazine", if you know what I mean'. I knew exactly what she meant and felt rather depressed.

Meanwhile, I have to report that Oscar and I had been rubbing away like mad with the magic cream for over a week now. She does it when I'm in the bath, and vice versa.

Neither of us has noticed any appreciable difference in the length of our clitorises (clitori?) but we're certainly having plenty of orgasms! In fact we find orgasms are quite easy to have provided there aren't any men around, doing all the wrong things.

We plan to do a little practical field work soon with the Norwegians, and have devised a code – O for orgasm, EO for enormous orgasm and NO for none. Oscar had an EO the other night, and practically fell out of bed.

Tuesday, 15th June

I made the fatal mistake of showing my poem to Hans.

'Why can't you give up this Bohemian shit and be a nice normal girl?' he asked, when he'd finished reading it.

We were lying on his bed at the Albert Hotel and I noticed his ears had gone pink, which is always a bad sign.

'I hope you won't mind my saying this, Jonnka, but really I don't understand this sort of stuff, and what's more I can't stand Bohemian girls. I don't like arty chaps much either – those creeps who wear berets and paint women with one eye in the middle of their foreheads!'

He swigged down a tooth glass of whisky – I have noticed he is drinking much more these days – and just to keep him company I swigged one too.

'But you must like *some* paintings!'

'Yes, of course – I like Rembrandt and that chap who paints sunflowers – a girlfriend of mine in Oslo had one over her bed – but apart from that, modern art makes me want to throw up.'

I was beginning to think that Hans and I didn't really have an awful lot in common. I tried to imagine being married to him, surrounded by muscular blondes who ski all the time and don't wear glasses and hate modern art – and awful meals with his mother who would probably dislike me. Shades of suburbia in Christiansand! The very thought of it made me reach for the whisky again. Maybe this love of ours is just some kind of sick aberration only made possible by the war? Maybe he only loves me because the crew love me – I'm one of the boys, I drink and say 'fy faen'!

Soon Danny and Otto joined us and announced that they wished to get seriously drunk. Hans sent them over to the boat for more bottles and told them to buy a few proper glasses from Woolworths. Then he turned the wireless on, lit his pipe and settled down, nice and comfortable, with his feet in the po cupboard, while I lay on the bed. The drinks arrived.

'And now,' he announced with an evil glint in his eye, 'we will see if you are truly a member of the flotilla, Joan. You will drink glass for glass with us until you either pass out, or sign a paper saying you surrender. You, Otto, will keep count.'

The drinks were poured and they were huge, like two doubles each, and soon we were all arguing and swearing and singing and dancing. My Norwegian became miraculously fluent. But I knew I couldn't take much more Scotch.

'So you surrender!' jeered Hans, waving a piece of paper at me, 'just like a bloody woman!'

This made me see red, so I wrote 'Never' with a shaking hand, downed a few more and shortly afterwards fell unconscious to the floor.

Four hours later I came round, and honestly no one could have been sweeter than those boys. One is always told men hate women who are drunk, but I don't agree – I think they like it, it makes them feel big, husky and protective or something. They carried me to the bathroom and held my head, washed my face and combed my hair – my God, I never felt so awful. I vaguely remember lying with my head on the WC seat moaning 'Go away, I want to sleep. I like this place.'

Poor Hans kept saying, 'Now then, Joanie, be a good girl and bring it up – don't mind me. Remember I'm your best friend.'

Since then I've been firmly on the wagon and I haven't written any more poetry either.

Wednesday, 16th June

Still feeling rather frail after this mammoth session with the Demon Alk. I made the mistake of describing the scene to my mother, and got a very shirty letter back accusing me of having an inward urge towards the sordid – inherited, no doubt, from my father. I didn't intend to let her get away with this, so replied as follows:

Darling Mama,

Thank you so much for sending me the tartan sewing thing, and the bear with pins for whiskers.

As for sordidness – I don't remember saying I particularly *enjoyed* that afternoon with the sailors. I just told you what happened, that's all. Actually, sordidness for its own sake leaves me cold, though I do sometimes like it when it's amusing. It's also fun in films or books, but a bit uncomfortable at close quarters.

As a matter of fact, if I *have* any 'inward urge' towards any-thing, it's towards that social life (of great respectability) which you seem to hate so much and which you deprived me of. If you really want to know, I've always secretly longed to be a deb!

Thank you very much for the Barlova drink, we have it with our hot milk at night and it's delicious. Thanks too for my new Polyfotos, they are very good indeed. I look like a choirboy that's gone wrong.

Everyone here seems to think I ought to marry Hans after the war. What do you think? I think it might be my salvation. Of course he hasn't asked me yet. Please pray that he gets the right idea soon and ask Sid to do the same.

Love,
Joan

Friday, 18th June

This morning I got a most unexpected phone call from Veronica inviting me to a cocktail party given by old Lady Lovat at the castle.

All the local lairds were invited, and tottered forth from their castles in kilt and sporran.

I was cornered by a quite fantastic roaring old Highland pansy called Major Monroe-Ferguson, the Oscar Wilde of the Highlands. He appeared to know my relations, and talked for ages about family trees. Apparently he is so mean that if you visit him at Novar Castle you have to bring your own sandwiches.

All the women seem to affect the same kind of headgear, an inverted felt porridge-bowl, with a moulting eagle's feather secured to it by the clan badge. I escaped the Major and stayed firmly by the food.

Hamish writes that he is due for leave soon. Strangely enough, although I love Hans the mere sight of Hamish's handwriting still sends tremors of excitement through me — I foresee fearful complications! Hans doesn't know about him yet, but I suppose I shall have to tell him one day. We only have a few days of the refit left.

Monday, 21st June

Today Hans actually had the nerve to ask me for that fiver back which I'd borrowed ages ago, when we were in London. Needless to say I was broke, but I was so cross and upset that I went straight to Mr Levine in the High Street and sold him my enamelled locket — the one I keep a lock of Hans's hair in.

When I got back to the Windsor I told Oscar all about it,

saying 'God, it was infuriating, I had to go to a Jew and sell my locket.'

Oscar looked at me coldly. 'Why do you use that word?' she said. 'Why not just say Mr Levine's shop? You know, I really hate the way you talk sometimes – about Jews and tarts and people being 'common'. I suppose it was just the rotten way you were brought up. I bet your mother thought servants were common and anyone wearing lipstick was a tart.'

I was very taken aback by this sudden attack. 'I don't know what you mean,' I said, 'it's only a word, isn't it? Everyone says "Jew" the way everyone says "Nigger". It's just an expression, meaning what they are.'

'It wasn't so much the word it was the way you said it. Did it ever occur to you that I'm Jewish?'

As a matter of fact it hadn't – not for one minute. It was our first row, and I felt awful, and apologised. Now I come to think of it, I *have* been brought up to think of Jews in a certain way: a very special sort of way and not a nice one.

Anyway, as it turned out the whole thing need never have happened because when I gave Hans the money he was aghast.

'You mean you sold your jewellery? For me? Surely not the locket I gave you! The one with my hair in it?'

When I said yes he went haring down to Levine's shop and bought it back!

24th June

Time is running out fast. Tonight I decided to make one last try for an O and persuaded Hans to bike miles down river, where we made love in a haystack – the setting was idyllic, still sunny at midnight with midges hanging in the air – but alas, NO.

Oscar also reports no progress with Danny. What a waste of thirty bob! We would have done better to have spent it on fish and chips. Still, it's been quite a lot of fun, though not of much practical use in the field.

Saturday, 26th June

This morning Oscar and I are sitting by our bedroom window moping. Our lovers leave on Monday. Pandora, who has a beautiful voice, is singing us German love songs which she learnt on holiday before the war:

> Ich hab' mein Herz in Heidelberg verloren,
> Es war ein schöner Sommer nicht.

We have succumbed to a phase which most girls get over when they are about fourteen – i.e., the wish to have been a boy and run away to sea.

Danny is still drinking, and Hans has fleas. He has to break off from passionate embraces to have a good scratch.

Sunday

Unfortunately all of us have now caught Hans's fleas and Pandora has to go to bed with great dignity in her oyster-grey satin pyjamas (Russian émigré style) with bicycle clips on the bottom to keep the fleas from climbing up her legs, just like she did at Preston. Of course the fleas aren't fooled and merely walk in the other end!

Tomorrow our boys sail for the Shetlands, and for months, maybe, they'll be docked in Lerwick. I don't know how often they go out to raid the Norwegian coast and torpedo German boats, but I do know it's bloody dangerous. I mean they're not like submarines that can disappear, they're a sitting duck for any Focke-Wulf that comes along. I'm hoping Hans will get his own boat soon and not have to take unnecessary risks with that crazy Danny any more.

Talking of Danny, he has rung up with a mysterious summons to attend a farewell party on the boat – he says there is a little surprise awaiting me!

That night

The ship was in the slips, freshly painted a beautiful green. Swans were swimming across the firth. I wore my slacks and a white blouse so as to look nautical.

The tiny wardroom was dominated by George, whose glassy eyes gazed down from the wall. He was wearing a sailor's cap, the light glistening on the jewels in his horns.

Down the middle was a very narrow table set with huge platters of salmon and boiled potatoes, and sauceboats of melted butter. As it was too small for both sides to eat off it at once, Danny got out his stopwatch, and every five minutes one side hauled the table towards them and the other had to eat off their laps. This led to an awful lot of melted butter ending up on my newly cleaned trousers.

Hans kept one arm firmly around me and ate with the other, while Danny embraced Oscar. We drank lots of very good old Graves, served by a Scottish rating, who adores working for the Norwegians, but thinks they are all mad. He pours the booze with a perpetual air of dour but benevolent amusement. Every now and then the huge blasphemous cook from Bergen would put his hairy head through the hatch, releasing a cloud of steam, swear hideously at us and bang it to again.

Oscar and I had made some cretonne curtains for the wardroom, so we hung them after dinner, then got down to serious drinking, i.e. whisky. Soon Hans whisked me up on to the bridge and we were playing at being Nelson at Trafalgar when we heard ominous sounds coming from below. Danny, a wild gleam in his eye, was raging around shouting his battle cry of 'Bang-bank-berserk!' and firing at the swans through the lavatory window with his Colt. Luckily he was too drunk to hit anything.

When we came down from the bridge he and Otto had their heads together and shortly afterwards they disappeared into the captain's cabin.

'What the hell's going on?' I asked Oscar.

'I shudder to think,' she said. 'They've been plotting for ages.'

Suddenly there was a sound of chanting and in came Danny dressed as a clergyman in a dog collar, bearing aloft a tome of navigational law, followed by Otto in stiff wing collar and bow tie. They were both beaming with anticipation and benevolence and very, very drunk.

'I am the Very Reverend Per Danielsen,' he chants, 'a Doctor of Divinity, and as Captain of this boat I'm going to marry you, Joan Wyndham, to Mr Hans Horatio Nelson Gundersen, the human torpedo – six feet of fighting manhood.'

'Fy til faen!' groaned Hans, eartips going bright pink.

'And I,' said Otto, stepping forward and seizing him firmly, 'am your best man.'

Before we knew where we were, Hans and I were kneeling at the table looking quite matrimonial in our white shirts. We borrowed a ring from Oscar, and made another from a twist of silver paper and Danny read the service from the navigational handbook.

Otto was called upon for a speech and gave a very moving and rather incoherent address to the young couple on the joys of married life. Poor Hans was a bit embarrassed but I was loving every minute of it.

While we were signing the register we discovered we needed another witness, so a drunken but charming engineer called Alexander Davidson was shanghaied from the docks and brought aboard. He agreed to sign after he had had his collar and tie removed and a bottle of Graves poured over his head.

Then came toasts, and everyone embraced and shook hands. Mr Davidson by now had become a trifle maudlin, and seizing my arm he hissed in my ear, 'Fur better nur wuss, I dinna hold wi' fuling!' Hans then kissed the bride passionately and presented her with a .45 pom-pom bullet as a wedding present.

The flotilla song was given a new verse which started 'Here comes Fru Gundersen' and as we were belting it out we were surprised by a visit from the second-in-command of the flotilla who had just flown down from the Shetlands. A very scared and sober little man suddenly found himself in a cabin full of howling lunatics who poured whisky down his throat and danced around him whooping like Indians.

How we got off is a merciful blank – the police arrived, apparently, and had to remove us. The next thing I can vaguely remember is bicycling madly up and down Ness Bank doing figures of eight and occasionally remarking to the onlookers that I was unconscious. Shortly afterwards I fell off and Oscar and Pandora picked me up and put me to bed.

Next morning I awoke with a terrible hangover. Was I in fact Fru Gundersen? Does the captain of a ship have the right to marry you? 'No,' Pandora said firmly, 'you have to be a certain number of miles out to sea.' Which rather disappointed me.

Hans and I said our final goodbyes outside the Windsor, both of us so hungover we could scarcely stand.

I had prepared myself so well for his departure that I was not too shaken at the time, but Hans took it very hard indeed. He gave me something wrapped up in brown paper, and said I must hang it in my room and think about him every time I looked at it and it would help to keep him safe.

When I finally undid it it turned out to be a skull and crossbones on a piece of black wood with 'death' written under it. Hans had always had it on his boat when he went into action. It didn't look much of a good luck charm to me but it went nicely with Pandora's sign in German saying 'It is forbidden to pee when the train is standing in the station'. Our room now has a lot of class.

I was on watch at midnight, but luckily Oscar had some Eno's and I drank half a pint of it with a couple of Benzedrine. Still felt a bit dizzy leaning over the gallery, and was relieved when a possible 'hostile' that showed up on the tube heading for Wick turned out to be a flock of geese!

Sunday, 4th July

I hardly had time to mope over Hans before I was sent off on a week's refresher course to Bawdsey in Suffolk to visit radar stations and generally bone up on our Filter Room 'gen'. I came with this nice crazy girl Zoe, who dances at parties.

We live in a huge, magnificent manor house with green turrets and a garden running down to the sea: it has tennis courts and landmines on the lawn. As there are only a few strands of wire round the mines you have to be jolly careful that you don't lose your ball! Overhead the Spitfires swoop through the blue sky with their lovely elliptical wings.

We have a very fierce WAAF commander called Flight Officer Sidebottom, BEM. Her aide is a certain A/S/O B. E. Ware. It's all rather intimidating. The male CO, on the other hand, is great fun and rather kinky. The other night after dinner he had us all sitting round in a circle scratching one another's heads — he said it was a clean version of something called a Daisy Chain, whatever that may mean.

Anyway, the course finally came to an end and we took the three-hour ferry to Felixstowe for a last splash at the Felix Hotel.

I was drinking at the bar with Zoe when we noticed a curious sight — a private soldier in uniform sitting in an alcove furiously writing in a notepad, with a long black cigarette holder clamped between his teeth.

'Good God,' Zoe exclaimed, 'I think I know that chap!' And she dashed over to speak to him.

Soon she came back with this tall, dark-haired, elegant-looking man, whom she introduced as Julian MacLaren-Ross. He bought us all double whiskies and behaved exactly like an officer. I asked him what he was writing and he said they were short stories about the war. He used to be in an Officers' Training Corps but now he hopes to get invalided out.

As we had all got a few free days at the end of the course we decided to go up to London together. Julian wants to see his publisher and visit a few Soho pubs.

Monday, 5th July

An amazing transformation in Private J. Ross. Gone was the awful pongo uniform and in its place was a cream corduroy jacket, teddy-bear coat and silver-mounted cane. He looked a real toff if a little frayed at the edges. He has told us to call him Jay because everybody else does.

On the way down in the train Jay took out a box of matches

and taught us to play something called the Match Game. After that he talked, all the way to London, about himself, his literary aspirations and the ghastly time he'd been having in the Suffolks.

London is trying to look a bit sprucer now with most of the rubble cleared away. Every month the raids get fewer and fewer. Only two hundred people were killed in England last month, and the general mood is cheerful.

On arrival Jay took us straight to the Fitzroy, where he proceeded to play the Match Game with some cronies in a corner. Zoe and I soon got bored with this and she said she knew a much better pub which was called the Wheatsheaf. We decided to jettison Jay, as we were a bit fed up with him — he is one of those people who talk an awful lot but never listen to a word you say.

After a quick look into the Burglar's Rest (no one there), Zoe marched us into the Wheatsheaf which was positively buzzing with strange, eccentric-looking people.

It was a warm, cosy place with green seating and tartan panels on the wall. I soon spotted quite a few people I knew, including good old Nina Hamnett who came padding up to me in her long, button-up shoes, and said she was glad to see I was in uniform and 'doing my bit'. I backed away hastily as she spits a bit through her front teeth. Subra was there too — Annie's boyfriend — looking exotic and oriental in his red scarf, and little Gerald Wilde who used to paint at my studio in Redcliffe Road, with his long raggedy overcoat, prehensile nose and wildly roving eyes. We talked nostalgically about the good old days and the wonderful stews I used to make. These brought such a yearning, hungry look into his eyes that I thought I'd better buy him a Scotch egg.

I was up at the bar ordering it when somebody pinched my bottom. I had always imagined — obviously wrongly — that because I was an officer I would never get my bottom pinched again, clad as it was in Mr Gieves's best blue serge, but I'd reckoned without the small tubby man with curly hair, lips like Michelin tyres and protuberant brown eyes.

'Pretty WAAF,' he breathed lasciviously, edging in to a bar stool beside me. 'What's your name?'

I said it was Joan, and what was his?

'I'm Dylan Thomas, and I'm fucking skint,' he said. 'Be a nice

Waafie and buy me another Special Ale.' I realised then who he was, the author of *Twenty-five Poems*, which I had recently been reading and found partly pure magic, and partly totally incomprehensible.

After I'd bought his drink we went over to a table where a young man called Ruthven Todd was sitting, a schoolmasterly fellow with a long pale face and square-rimmed spectacles. He had a very loud voice and turned out to be yet another person who talked a lot and didn't listen.

My fascinated gaze was soon wandering around the room, thinking how much I'd missed Bohemian people. Ruthven interrupted my thoughts.

'Don't bother with that lot,' he said firmly, 'Tambi will touch you for a fiver, Subra will want to stand you on your head and make love to you in all sorts of weird, oriental positions, and as for Dylan he's a lovely man, but not safe after six.'

Zoe meanwhile was being mesmerised in a corner by this man called Tambi, an Indian with soft, dark hair and pouting lips, whose mauve pointed tongue flickered in and out of his mouth like a chameleon's.

'The booze is running out here,' Ruthven said, 'let's go to the Café Royal and have some of the real stuff, before my ulcer starts playing up.'

After half an hour in a back bar which seemed to stock unlimited Irish whisky, both my escorts were extremely whizzed.

Leaving the Café Royal we linked arms and charged up the narrow staircase leading to the Arts Theatre Club. We were instantly spotted by reception and it was a right turn, down the stairs and out into St Martin's Lane in five minutes flat. It seems that it is not 'Ah, here comes Dylan, that promising young poet!' but 'Watch out, here comes that crashing old bore Dylan, let's get him out of here quick.'

Just then the air-raid siren went off. We hailed a taxi and persuaded the driver to take us to Ruthven's studio. As soon as I'd sunk into my seat Dylan smothered me in wet beery kisses, his blubbery tongue forcing my lips apart. It was rather like being embraced by an intoxicated octopus. I tried to tell myself that I was being kissed by a great poet but it was a relief when the taxi finally stopped.

Ruthven's studio is stacked with books and when I told him I'd never read James Joyce's *Work in Progress*, he rooted around among the shelves and began to throw books at me with both hands. 'Here's *Anna Livia*, signed by the author, and a nice little limited edition of *Havers Childers*. Take them, take them. You can bring them back any time you want.'

There were bombs going off quite near, the first for a long time. We had beer and liver sausage on the floor and as it was late and the raid still on, Ruthven told me I could sleep on a mattress in his spare room, which was about the size of a cupboard.

I was just dozing off when someone fumbled with the lock and I could hear a hypnotic chant of 'I want to fuck you! I want to fuck you!' Quick as a flash I bolted the door and wedged a heavy armchair under the handle.

There were ominous thuds as Dylan hurled himself against the panelling. Thump went Dylan! Crump went the bombs!

I cowered miserably on the mattress. At last I heard Ruthven's voice firmly remonstrating, and finally the sounds of a heavy body being dragged reluctantly away.

I curled myself up under my greatcoat and slept like the dead.

Tuesday, 6th July

This morning it was as if nothing had ever happened. A sober and well-mannered cherub with pink and freshly shaven jowls and hardly a trace of a hangover knocked on my door and suggested that we go out for breakfast as Ruthven was working.

'There's a very good place for coffee just off Wardour Street,' he said. 'They have bloody good croissants.'

I was delighted as I had had nothing but a liver sausage sandwich since yesterday morning. We settled down in front of long glasses of milky coffee. After a bit he said, 'Do you mind if we have a few more croissants?'

At this point I realised that I was paying for the breakfast, and hurriedly fumbling in my shoulder bag, found to my relief that I had four bob.

He asked me to give Zoe his love, and tell her his new daughter is called Eiron. He says he is missing his wife Caitlin terribly.

We got on to the subject of work and discussed his poems, and I said there were an awful lot of lines I couldn't understand.

'Oh,' said Dylan, 'I shouldn't worry too much about that. It's like a walled city with many gates, it doesn't really matter which door you go in by – in fact it doesn't matter a tinker's toss if you don't go in at all.'

He lit another cigarette from the stub of the last one. 'Do you mind if we have another cup of coffee and change the subject? I really can't stand it when people ask me questions about my writing, I'm like those birds that eat their young when they're disturbed. Anyway, poetry is not the most important thing in life, is it? Frankly, I'd much rather lie in a hot bath sucking boiled sweets and reading Agatha Christie, which is just exactly what I intend to do as soon as I get home.'

I said I enjoyed that too, only with me it was Mars bars and Maldorer. He told me I was a dreadful literary snob and we parted most amicably, after I'd settled the bill.

Dylan, it seems, is really terribly nice provided you only see him in the mornings.

It was a relief to get back to my mother's flat, so clean and cosy. With two more free days in London, I'd decided it was time to catch up on my past, so rang Petya who seemed thrilled at the thought of having lunch with me. Also Rupert, and arranged to meet him later for drinks at the Nelson in the King's Road.

Meanwhile my mother had trotted off to Tulleys to buy herself three yards of silk to make herself a flea bag. She is spending quite a lot of nights now at the Casualty Post and has been bitten all over. The raids are much fewer, but still quite a few casualties.

I noticed a very funny note in the kitchen from old Kate who 'does' for my mother. 'Madam,' it said, 'had one at the top of our street. I was shot out of my bed. It was gastley, all night digging. Today I am nearly a cripple, I can hardly walk. It think it must be rumatism. I am breaking up. The butcher has run out of sausages.' My mother's note for today simply said, 'Dear Kate, so glad you are still alive. I think we will have Welsh Rarebit tonight.'

Stuffed heart at the British Restaurant. Petya moody. When I commented on it he replied magnificently that the whole second act of *Faust* was being enacted in his brain and guts.

He is thin and pale, hasn't a penny in the world and has been living on bread for a fortnight, so I gave him a good lunch. He has decided to become what he calls a 'serious craftsman' and has even given up wearing corduroy trousers.

Drinks at the Swiss where I became happy and drunk, holding Petya's hand and telling him I really loved him. Petya adores me when I'm drunk. I wish I was drunk always. We gazed into each other's eyes and relived the dramas of the past. I think if I were always drunk, I would be a much nicer person.

Suddenly Petya leapt up and said, 'Oh, good, there's Dylan, he owes me £5.' Later he brought him over to my table and said, 'I must introduce you to Joan – don't you think she's beautiful?' which I thought was rather funny seeing that Dylan had spent the whole of last night hurling himself against my bedroom door.

Drinks at the Coffee 'An which was full of pansies, ponces, poets and painters – lots of whom came up and talked to me. Petya says if I didn't wear trousers people wouldn't take me for a Chelsea tart.

Went out to Rupert's place at six, when I knew Annie would be out at her First Aid Post. He leant out of the top window and waved and laughed and threw me down the key. He seemed delighted to see me.

I went upstairs and there was the old double bed, the same one I had trundled through the streets after the bomb, and Rupert just up after one of his 'little snoozes', his hair tousled into curls, laughing and crowing 'I'm as mad as the noon-day sun'. We were very friendly and there was no embarrassment talking about old times in Redcliffe Road.

'What fun it all was,' I said.

'Yes – you know I really enjoyed it too. I found it quite exciting to take out an unsophisticated girl who hadn't seen it all before. How long ago that seems.' I asked about my old friend Prudey from Redcliffe Road and he said, 'Oh, didn't you know? She jumped out of a window – or maybe she just fell, you know how short-sighted she was.' Poor darling Prudey, I felt like crying, but couldn't in front of Rupert.

He wanted to play billiards so we went to the Six Bells, and there was Gerhardt with his new American girlfriend, Louise. He was wearing a white silk scarf tucked into the neck of his ARP tunic, and was pulling faces at himself in the glass, holding his head poised very high and slightly to one side.

'He's been like this for a long time,' Rupert said. 'Ever since Louise told him he had the best profile in London. It must give him an awful crick in the neck.'

Annie came in off watch, and joined us. I felt no jealousy at all, in fact I felt quite warm towards her. She was wearing a black and yellow open-neck silk shirt over her ARP trousers and seemed to have lost weight.

We sat in the corner drinking pink gins, and Rupert and Annie were playing a game called 'Rude Bears'. Gerhardt watched them through narrowed eyes, a cynical smile playing on his lips.

'Come into the nursery, Gerhardt!' Rupert cackled. Gerhardt merely flared his nostrils and tossed them a penny. Then we all went off to the Café Bleu for dinner with Quentin Crisp, our divine, red-headed neighbourhood pansy.

It felt very strange, being with the old gang again. Apart from Gerhardt, who is even more paranoid than before, they don't seem to have changed at all. I, on the other hand, feel a totally different person, less naive, and less tolerant of stupid childish behaviour. A bit more priggish, perhaps. Still, I'm very fond of Rupert, and always will be.

Wednesday, 7th July

On the last day I went round to see my old lesbian flame, Laura Napier. She has been in bed for six months now with TB, and looks lovely beyond all words, lying in bed with her blonde hair in a tangle round her face. Why does TB give people such marvellous complexions? She seemed so sane and nice.

We talked for hours about poetry and men and mothers and I loved being with her, just looking at her. Toni De Vaz has painted a wonderful portrait of her whilst she is lying in bed ill.

Lunch with Zoe and Augustus John at the Queen's Restaurant in Sloane Square. He is a lovely rugged bear of a man, even if he does try to have affairs with all his daughters. Zoe and I drank a bottle of white wine each and caught the train back to Scotland fairly whizzed.

Thursday, 8th July

INVERNESS

I have found a hive of trouble awaiting my return. Apparently the head WAAF in our job – the appalling Gloves – put in an adverse report on me and my work while I was away. I had to go and see the Group Captain on the afternoon that I arrived to read and initial it. I found that while all the other Commanding Officers had put fairly decent reports in, Gloves had put that I was a very peculiar type of officer, not amenable to discipline and a bad example to the other ranks!

Secretly I rather agreed with her, especially after my behaviour with the Norwegians, but I told the Group Captain that it was all balls, and he was perfectly charming and agreed with me. He is a typical officer type, very handsome and refined – about fifty – and he prides himself on being a judge of character. I very soon got his measure and decided to act very ladylike, put on plenty of pale powder, and after that it was a piece of cake. When Gloves was called on to appear, wearing gold earrings and masses of make-up, I could see the Group Captain quailing in his chair.

Anyhow, he asked her to substantiate her accusations and all she could say was that I had never actually disobeyed an order of hers or acted in any way contrary to discipline, but that she just didn't like the way I walked around and the way I looked at her – 'dumb insolence' she called it!

Well, the GC just sighed deeply and dismissed us, but as we

were going down the corridor Gloves hissed at me, 'You haven't heard the last of this, Wyndham!'

The report finally came back for me to initial, with the Group Captain's own remarks on it, i.e. the whole thing was far too severe, and he didn't consider me the least bit a peculiar type of officer, and that any faults I might have were not caused by innate idleness or disobedience but by lack of the right guidance from my superior officers! This made Gloves even more furious but everybody else is delighted.

Friday, 20th August

In spite of Gloves's bad report, I have been promoted to Flight Officer! *Two* thin bands, and a bit more pay too. So I am feeling pretty cheerful.

Poor Pandora, on the other hand, is getting more and more depressed as her married man has now been sent overseas. She boasts that she is so thin she can hold her bottom in the palm of one hand. I, unfortunately, get larger every day, making up for Hans's absence with fish and chips. I think I have put on seven pounds since he went back to the Shetlands!

Yesterday, after supper, Pan and I biked up to the head of Loch Ness and sat on the beach looking down the loch to the setting sun. It was quite perfect, the sky had turned the water the colour of pink champagne, all transparent and glowing, from the waves at our feet to where the mountains met the mist on the horizon.

Riding home we caught a whiff of that gorgeous scent that means wild raspberries – happily we found a nice big patch which we devoured like locusts.

Sunday, 22nd August

Oscar is very keen to meet the Lovats, having heard so much about them, so I'm taking her over to the island today. Veronica drove us there and by chance a very nice man called Stefan Zeizel was staying in the house. He is a brilliant pianist, an Austrian Jew who spent three years in Dachau.

Oscar seemed totally fascinated by him, they spent an awful lot of time talking to each other in corners. I couldn't hear what they were saying, but it seemed to have a strange effect on Oscar, who became very quiet and subdued.

For lunch we had a very good wine called La Joyeuse, and then a serf entered bearing no less than four roast chickens on a silver platter – for six people! As usual, I ate like a pig, but Oscar seemed to have totally lost her appetite.

Over pudding, which was a sort of uncooked chocolate cake with biscuits in it (called Petworth Pudding), Mam'zelle, their old French governess, regaled us with her life history, vividly recounted with much Gallic gesticulation. She is one of those dear, prim, innocent creatures to whom everything happens, floods, earthquakes in Brazil, shipwreck among electric eels, homicidal maniacs in trains, sex-mad dentists who attack her while under the drill, etc. I laughed till I cried; her reactions to all these *affreux* happenings were so perfectly in character.

In the afternoon we went swimming with Veronica and the children, clambering down a steep rock face to a little cove of white sand by huge waterfalls. The water was brown like sherry and the sand hot and white. The only way we could get up enough courage to immerse ourselves was by wriggling like seals down the beach and gradually lowering our solar plexuses into the icy water.

Later we had a huge picnic tea, and staggered home drunk like bees on bread, honey and sunshine.

Before we left Stefan played the piano for us. Bach fugues and Mozart sonatas, and a lovely lute song by Dowland called 'Weep Ye No More Sad Fountains' which I sang, very badly.

To my delight Hamish rang while I was there, and asked to speak to me – can I join him in London on a forty-eight-hour pass some time early in September? I am like putty as soon as I hear his voice, in spite of guilty thoughts about Hans.

Back to the Mess laden with eggs and flowers, white roses, purple pansies and yellow lilies.

As Oscar was putting them into vases on our windowsill I asked her why she seemed so quiet, and what had Stefan been saying to her.

'He told me a lot of terrible things. It is much, much worse in the camps than we ever imagined. Do you realise what they are doing to children in Dachau?' She went on to tell me stories, things I could hardly believe, but Stefan has seen it with his own eyes. It made me feel quite sick with anger.

Later I could hear Oscar crying in the night.

Monday, 6th September

LONDON

Hamish rang. I got my two-day pass, and we met in the Ritz bar. He looked so handsome in his black beret, I was quite bowled over.

Veronica had lent me a hat for the Ritz. It is an enormous pink rose set in green leaves and has to be perched hazardously over one eye with the aid of a few kirbigrips. Hamish took one look at it and said, 'You know, I'm not quite sure about that hat!' So I dashed into the powder room and took it off. I was amazed at my reflection. My skin glowed and I looked lovely. I think I am getting much better-looking these days.

When I got back to the table H had ordered partridges, which was unfortunate as they are not the sort of thing you can very easily eat if you want to look glamorous at the same time. However, I fluttered my eyelashes and did my little girl act, all naive and wide-eyed.

'Oh, partridges! I don't think I've ever had them before!'

'Look, Sweetie,' Hamish said wearily, 'you are overdoing it a bit, aren't you? I mean the "Little Alice in Aristoland" number. Of course you've had partridges before.'

'Well once,' I admitted, 'when I was only six, in a gamekeeper's cottage, and I broke my tooth on some shot, so I've never eaten them again.'

It wasn't a very good meal as I had to worry about continuing to look attractive. Uninhibited chewing is out, and you can't really relax and enjoy your grub under these conditions.

He could see I was miserable picking at the tiny carcasses, so he ordered me oysters and Chablis instead, which was much better, and soon I was enjoying every minute of it. I loved the way the waiters were all fussing around our chairs, unfolding napkins, removing totally clean ashtrays, moving up phalanxes of crisp hot toast and butter curls – all that wonderful performance that means that they intend to shake you down for a cool fiver. But Hamish seemed quite unimpressed and very much at home. He says he wants to make me into a smartie. What a hope!

I felt like dancing, so we went to Hatchetts, and pranced around to 'Besame Mucho' and 'Pistol Packin' Mama', and everybody sang and we were madly happy.

'We're horribly alike, you know,' Hamish said as we sank back into our seats, 'tastes, character, everything – we even like the same tunes. And our weaknesses – the way we can't be really fond of people.'

Speak for yourself, I thought.

'However,' he went on, 'you're not a shit like me – a sensual, arrogant bastard who shouldn't be making love to a girl he doesn't mean to marry. You're such a sweetie-pie and I'm such a shit.'

After that the fun seemed to have gone out of the evening. I know I shouldn't have felt hurt but I did.

Later, in bed in his hotel, I just lay beside him and hugged him comfortably, and told him to forget about this damn silly love-making business. I realised what a mistake it had been, sleeping with him in the first place, and luckily I had the Catholic church as an excuse. I didn't really want to tell him about Hans.

'You're a funny girl,' he said, 'you're terribly attractive but not the least bit amorously inclined.'

Wednesday, 8th September

Back to Inverness on the morning train feeling empty and depressed. This affair with Hamish is getting me nowhere.

Next day I rang up Veronica, who volunteered to cheer me up. We had a beautiful lunch ending with saucer pancakes, and played Mozart on the gramophone.

I tried to tell her about Hans, but she still firmly believes I ought to marry old Hamish. She says I'm the only one of his girls she ever liked, and the only one who didn't bore him to tears. She believes we would make each other blissful.

Mama writes that she has to fire-watch on top of Nell Gwyn House and she is terrified and will I send her some Benzedrine! I felt quilty for not seeing her when I was in London and wrote back right away.

Darling Mama,

Just got your letter telling of fearful experience with the fire bombs – how I feel for you! I think it is absolutely monstrous that you should have to go out on the roof for fire-watching!

I think I had better send you a Benzedrine prescription of your own soon. Or maybe Mr Steele across the road would give you one – why don't you ask him?

As for me and Hamish, we are still very good friends, but you must put out of your mind any thought of our getting married. In the first place I don't really love him, and this thing of marrying for position is all very well but I think I would very soon get fed up with the 'grand life'. Also, although H is not bored with me now, I know he soon would be. He's one of the most easily bored people in the world. So you can put it right out of your mind.

Veronica, however, is a great matchmaker, and we have the most extraordinary conversations.

'Well, if you don't fancy Hamish how about the Oxford and Asquith boy?'

'But, Veronica, he hasn't a great deal of sex appeal, has he?'

'No, darling, but he's got a "seat" – a beautiful place called Mells – and he's a good Catholic and a dear sweet scholarly boy.'

It seems you can't be too fussy when hooking an earl!

Anyway, Mum, I'm cheesed — I want a husband — in fact, I shall probably marry the next chap who asks me, provided he's kind and rich, funny and likes children.

Hans still writes that he loves me madly, which is nice to know, but I'm still cheesed.

Could you send me the Arden powder in the pink cardboard box, and my gold Cherry Yardley lipstick?

Bugger the bombs — enclose Benzedrine!

Love,

Joan

Hans has written me a letter that starts off quite boring and normal, and then goes off the rails. 'I don't bloody hell know why but there is so much I'd wish I could write to you, but I shall get drunk one day and then you shall get a long, long letter! Probably only nonsense but I shall write that I love you on every line. Now I am writing it only once time: I love you so damn much my little one.'

I think part of his passion for me must be due to the awful boredom of life on Shetland, not to mention the shortage of girls. Danny once told me that up there you are either bored, drunk, cold or randy — usually all four. No wonder Hans misses me!

We've only been to one decent dance recently, given by the 52nd Division at Craigellachie, General Ritchie's lot.

I was monopolised by a frightfully blasé London type (ah, the good old days when we all lived on Pernod and Benzedrine!). Then the colonel steamed up for an eightsome reel — a huge magnificent man in a kilt who charged around the floor like a Churchill tank.

There was only one sticky moment, when 'the scrubbah's daughter, by gad!' turned up in a dress of the same viridian green as the colonel's wife. (The scrubber is the chap who goes round in a van giving baths to soldiers.)

Next morning we drove back through fifty miles of heavenly country, along the river Spey, between mountains whose colour was like the bloom on a grape.

Friday, 26th November

We are busy getting our Christmas presents ready for the Norwegians. I've made up a huge parcel for the ship wrapped in tartan paper and one of our Fleet Air Arm boys will fly it up next week. A Dunhill pipe for Hans, plus expensive tobacco, and a book on Van Gogh to improve his mind. For Danny I've got a cat mascot, and a large bottle of Eno's. I filled the crevices with holly and mistletoe and tied it up with tinsel.

25th December

On Christmas Day I wore my white evening dress with silver earrings. We had decorated the old Operations block to look like a West End restaurant, with little tables in the balcony and Joe Daniels's band. There was turkey and plum pudding, passing the port to the left, and much singing of 'The Virgin Sturgeon' and 'Roll Me Over in the Clover', followed by carols.

Zoe put on her flame-coloured skirt and her usual mad Hungarian dance, which ended with her running the full length of the room and hurling herself to the floor at the CO's feet, her hair tossed forward over her face. The CO looked most embarrassed.

I danced with a veritable waltzing mouse of a fighter pilot called 'Guns' — terribly sweet, lovely teeth but with the brains of a newt. Nothing to say but Whizzo-O and Bang-On. He told me he'd love to have me for a sister.

It snows almost every day now, alternating with blue skies, very cold and clear. At New Year there was a dance given by the 1st Suffolks where there were oysters and hot punch *and* four men to every girl. I got kissed by twenty men!

5th January 1944

Hans's Xmas letter finally arrived – he is miserable without me and life is hell, which is most gratifying to hear. He says he wanted to ring me on Christmas morning, but knew it would only make him more miserable. 'I damned well agree with you,' he writes, 'we had some jolly good times together. Times that mean a lot more to me now than when it all happened. Everything up here is so bloody boring and makes me to long for you like hell.

'I once told you I didn't think I ever loved anybody. I hope you excuse me when I term it love, always to want to be with you when I'm away from you. I sincerely love you, my darling.'

Petya's letter arrived in a dead heat. My rather rash Xmas card to him (horse and foal, 3½d.) had evoked 'a warm vagrant melancholy like the boiling wine of the Carpathian mountains'. He says he is still ill and starving and spent his last 3d. in the world on a stamp for my letter.

Hans's parcel has also just arrived, hand-knitted Shetland jumper which everybody loves but I am a bit dubious about – it is v. loud! Also five pairs of silk stockings, and some silky material in a rather unpleasant electric blue which I intend to dye. Veronica knows a little woman who could have it made up for me, she only charges £1.

I now have to write and thank Mama for her Christmas parcel of mixed blessings.

Darling Mama,

I hope Xmas was as happy for you as it was for me. Thank God the raids have abated.

Hans adored the Dunhill pipe and we are saving your peaches and brandy for a grand occasion.

I think the lavender-bag is awfully pretty and the stuffed cat for Danny was a masterpiece, but my dear, the belt! I was so horrified I nearly fell through the lavatory seat on which I happened to be sitting at the time of opening your parcel. However, I have dyed it black with ink and boot polish. It will go all right with my slacks on watch, I think. Anyhow, thank you very much all the same – ha ha.

The Jaeger pyjamas are wonderful and just the right shade of peacock blue. All of the girls in my Mess want to borrow them for dirty weekends, which I think is a bit much as they are all nice 'gels'. And some of them are virgins! Still I suppose they will go over the edge soon whether they borrow my pyjamas or not.

Thanks too for the second lot of Polyfotos. They are v. strange and I am quite obviously in love in every one of them. I look intense, lopsided, *spirituelle* and boss-eyed. In one or two of them I appear to be about to receive the stigmata.

Hamish has sent me an amazing photo of himself – what is known as 'boudoir size', I believe. He looks a complete upper-class bounder, with pin-striped suit, flowing silk tie, oiled hair, quirked eyebrow and crocodile smile. From a black enamelled frame with gold flowers (6d. second-hand) he leers down from my mantelpiece, the pride and joy of all beholders.

My white dress was a roaring success over Christmas in spite of mothholes. Could you please patch my cream lace blouse under the arms and ask Kate to wash it and starch it very slightly?

Lots of love,
Joan

15th January

Three tedious weeks have passed since Christmas, and no word from Hans. I am beginning to get very worried. Every day I wander down to the Cally bar to see if I can pick up any news from the Norwegians there.

Today I met Hans's friend Sandstorm, and he said that the last he heard was some weeks ago – the flotilla had made five attempts at a raid on the Norwegian coast but always had to return as it was too light. The last time they were chased by a Focke-Wulf, a Junker and a Blohm and Voss and promptly shot down all three!

Sandstorm stood me a cheering G & T and I sent yet another wire to Lerwick from the post office. Half the time I'm hopeful, the rest I think he is dead for sure. Mainly because he is on Danny's boat and therefore more at risk.

Thursday

Sandstorm told me today that one of the boats had sunk a big merchantman but he doesn't know which. He thinks that Otto has been wounded in the leg but no news of Hans. Sent another wire. Still no answer. The Wrens are trying to get some info for me this morning.

I love him like hell and I feel quite ill with worry, the most bloody awful weeks of my life. I think I've aged about ten years. Serve me right for mooning after Hamish.

5th February

I haven't eaten for two days. After a night of bad dreams I crawled wearily down to see if I could swallow some breakfast and there was this amazing drunken letter. I laughed and cried like hell. His writing was almost unreadable but in the end I managed to make it out.

Beloved Joan,
I never died! However being away from you is a living death! I am drunk! Drunk! Very jolly drunk!

But in my drunken heart your sober picture glows as always, you bloody bastard! I love you as distracted – I will be down to you soon, I hope.

Later: I am still drunk! I never fucked anybody up here! I haven't! Oh God, I wish I had you! I take sherry. Still drunk.

My gorgeous woman! – more sherry – I want you night and day. I need you, with dreams haunting my sleep, to have you here, to feel you here – oh maddening thought, it makes me
xxxxxxxx————xxxxxxxx !!!! ????????

Darling Joan, Jenta me, I am so bloody fond of you. As ever, now and in eternity.

Yours,
Hans

This was probably the nicest letter I had ever received in my life, and I was so crazy with relief that it gave me the most wonderful appetite for breakfast. I really do think I ought to marry him after the war. It would be the salvation of me, apart from the fact that I love him like hell.

Tuesday, 15th February

Had a lovely weekend with Veronica, we cooked the most amazing meals and ate them by the drawing room fire. There seems to be an endless supply of homemade butter and cream. The best thing we made was something called *pain perdu*, which is bread fried in syrup and eaten with cream – delicious!

We talked about Hamish and how he has had it in for Shimi ever since he, Hamish, brought back a load of flamenco records from Spain and went to stay at the castle. After he'd played them day and night for a few days, Shimi got a bit fed up, took a rook rifle and the records up to the highest turret and ordered a ghillie to chuck them in the air for target practice.

At night V lent me one of her gorgeous trousseau nightdresses in pink chiffon, and a lace negligée to go over it, with ermine slippers.

I slept in a flower-papered room in a little four-poster bed with fluted pillars, full of pot-pourri and lilies of the valley. Next morning I came down to breakfast in my negligée, looking like the Queen of Sheba, and ate porridge and cream with the children out of wooden bowls. They are lovely kids, like Walt Disney angels. No news of Veronica's husband, alas, who is still missing.

On my last day, we went to the castle to see Rosie's new gun-dog puppies, and hutches of white ferrets with blood-red eyes. The gamekeeper calls them 'varmints', lovely, evil-looking beasties, one of which bit me to the bone. When I see beautiful animals my whole heart goes out to them, I admire them frantically for looking so handsome, and doing everything so rightly and well – and also for having had the good sense not to be humans!

Then to the walled garden to cut cabbages where we were accosted by a D. H. Lawrence character in moleskins with a gun and a liver-and-white bitch.

'I'm coom to shoot the rabbit in the garden,' he said, giving me a deep, dark, earthbound look, and vanished into the shrubbery. I fled with my fingers in my ears, pursued by the sound of shattering explosions.

Nevertheless it was a lovely restful weekend, and I really needed it as we're frightfully busy on watch nowadays. Our bombers are out night after night, dropping thousands of tons on Germany and on the V-bomb launching sites.

Pandora's weekend was not such a success. She had departed for the Drumnadrochit Hotel with the Canadian colonel who had suddenly appeared on leave, finally determined to lose her virginity – not, thank God, in (or out of) my new Jaeger pyjamas. However, she got cold feet and locked her door when the crunch came.

Hamish writes from the Army School for Poison Gas in Salisbury. 'To be a student is bad enough,' he says, 'but military student life is intolerable – and of all the jolly military curriculi, what brighter subject than poison gas?'

Thursday, 23rd March

At 7 a.m. Danny brought MTB 718 roaring down the Caledonian Canal doing 30 knots, which is faster than a train. The maximum speed allowed is 3 knots!

Oscar and I had come back exhausted after night watch and were resting on our beds, having a nice peaceful read, when a distressed orderly rushed in. There were, she said, two gentlemen below, determined to come up to our bedroom.

'What do they look like?' we asked with a sudden flash of hope.

'Well,' she said, 'one of them looks all right, apart from having his arm in a sling, but the other's dead drunk and he's wearing a black patch over one eye and carrying a shepherd's crook. He says he must see you because all of your relatives have been killed in a bomb and he's your last remaining brother.'

At this point the orderly was swept aside, and our two brave boys roared in merry and tight and swept us off the beds into their arms. Hans looked red and weather-beaten and very thin, with his arm in a sling, and Danny looked outrageous as ever. Apparently he fought a commando on Shetland, hence the sprained ankle and black eye. He has cut a patch for it from a pair of his old shoes.

I asked them where they were staying and Danny said that no hotel would have him or even serve him a drink. I think it's absolutely disgusting that old Danny, who is a positive hero, with more gongs than will fit on his jacket, should be barred by these bloody civilians!

Later we all met up at the Cally. Hans has brought me a present from London, a terrible old moleskin muff with tails on it. They bought it for a colossal sum in Harrod's when they were drunk, and I had to pretend to be highly delighted.

He looks terribly operational now that he has his own boat and wears a floppy cap encrusted with barnacles. He seems to have grown up a bit, more like a man now than a boy.

'You know,' Hans said, 'that time you thought I was dead? Well you must be telepathic or some bloody thing. There was this heavily escorted battleship and I was sent out on an English boat to sink it. "You haven't a chance in hell," says this old bastard at the briefing office. "One-way petrol only!"

'Well I don't mind dying with my old friends, but not with a bunch of bloody Scotsmen! Anyway we were recalled within half an hour of the target and I cried with relief and got drunk as a skunk. And those other silly buggers – do you know what they said? "Damn poor show!"'

Danny was not there, he had fled to the mountains with a blonde and found some hotel that hadn't heard of him (yet), so I had dinner with Hans and dear old Otto who was on crutches.

It didn't take me long to realise that something was niggling Hans. Once we got back to the Albert he got rid of Otto on some pretext and began to question me jealously about Hamish, who I had rather rashly mentioned in my letters. Was I in love with him, how often did I see him? I explained that he was away most of the time on highly secret duties and anyway he was more like a friend of the family, a relative actually.

Hans reached for the whisky. 'You shoot the line a bit?' I tried to reassure him but his mood was black. I've never seen him so intense and neurotic.

'I wish I'd never met you,' he muttered. 'I never meant to fall in love with a bloody English girl – always before I avoid them. I've seen it before, what a mistake it is to marry them. But you! I hate you and I love you, you're a bloody devil and I'll kill you one day, by God!'

Friday, 24th

No word from Hans after yesterday's row.

I wandered disconsolately down to the slipway to see if he was there. I could see Danny's boat with a freshly painted, white swastika on the front of it for their last kill. The old boy by the gate knows me by now so he let me through and I found Danny back from the mountains, tidying up the mess in his cabin.

'I'm living here now,' he said. 'Nowhere else will have me!'

He brought out a bottle of something curiously potent called Algerian vin d'Oran. There was no water laid on so we washed the glasses in gin. He could see I wanted to talk about Hans and decided to give me some good advice.

'You know, Jonnka, you don't really know this boy – you think he has the nature of an angel, but I tell you he is far tougher than I am, especially now he has his own command. Now me, I am delicate like a French dog, sick for days after a sinking – when I see tracer bullets coming I feel like fainting! But Hans – I remember that time the Germans were in the water and we went full speed ahead with our propellers. The Germans went into our propellers – Hans said it was so "bee-yootiful"!'

I hastily drank some more red vinegar to hide my dismay, and lit another black and gold Russian Sobranie, the kind that Hans hates because he suspects them of being Bohemian.

'And as for marriage!' Danny went on. 'Olaf and all the other boys think you should marry Hans – they take it for granted. I, on the other hand, think you are the types who would make hell for each other ninety-eight days out of a hundred.'

'I wish I were a man,' I said wearily. 'Then I could be Hans's friend and join the flotilla, and there wouldn't be any problems!'

'Ja visst, a month in the wardroom of 718 would do you all the good in the world – but give Hans a rest for a while. He is not in a good mood.'

Went on watch at midnight feeling miserable. It seems my angelic Hans is a bit of a devil after all. The trouble is I don't know how long I can bear to keep away from him.

Saturday, 25th

Spent the morning telling myself that I would not ring Hans or go to see him, spent the afternoon crying, and by six o'clock I was at the Albert Hotel.

I went straight up to his room and entered without knocking. Danny and Otto were there with him and the wastepaper basket was entirely filled with empty bottles of gin, whisky and Norwegian punch. They had been drinking punch laced with gin and looked as though they had been doing it for quite a long time. 'Vi er fylle som kaskaneene!' Danny said happily, meaning they were drunk as a barrelful of rabbits. Hans doesn't usually drink as much as the others but I realised that this time he was blind roaring stinko.

'Aha,' he said when he saw me come in. 'So here you are! And who were you sleeping with last night?'

Danny got off the bed to leave and Otto reached for his crutches. 'I think,' said Danny, 'that we had a date in Cally Hotel, no?'

'Maybe I'll join you,' I said, feeling rather scared, but Hans seized me by the throat and hurled me back on to the bed.

'Oh no you don't,' he said, 'now that you're here you might as well join me!'

Before he left, Otto very tactfully turned the radio on extremely loud. Hans lurched groggily off his bed, poured punch into a tooth glass and tried to pour it forcibly down my throat. I knocked it out of his hand and it splashed all over the room.

Then I tried to make a run for the door but before I could reach the handle Hans knocked me to the ground with a flying left. I got to my feet and broke several records over his head, one of which I recollect was called 'Apple Blossom and Chapel Bells'. To my amazement he burst into tears. Tearful and apologetic, he spent the next quarter of an hour with his head on my breast, informing me that he was in love with a torpedo.

'Take the most beautiful woman in the whole world, take music, take Rembrandt and Van Gogh, but give me a Mark 9 two-star magnetic torpedo! Ah Joan, I love it. It's human, alive, like a person. It finds its own way through the water.' And so on and so on, ad nauseam. After torpedoes he progressed to destroyers which he adores too – all this I could put up with but when he started on how he loved killing Germans and how great it was to watch a fifty-foot depth charge blow the guts out of them in the water, I knew it was time to go. I've never met anyone who hates the Germans the way he does. That – and his love of ships – are like a religion to him.

Anyway the whole thing was profoundly boring and I ran downstairs with Hans following after.

As soon as the cold air hit him he went berserk, and I had to slap his face. He slapped me back in the middle of the road, unfortunately in full view of some of my own WAAFs who were standing outside their hostel. Then he got a grip on my throat. I struggled to escape and he began to throw me around like a rag doll amid cheers from nearby Cameron Highlanders. When I tried to break free he bit me in the hand and drew blood – my neck and face were covered in bruises and the badge had been torn clean off my hat.

This lasted all the way to the Windsor Hotel where, luckily, we were met by three more Norwegians who rescued me and carried me at a run down the road with my legs in the air. I screamed and struggled and my cap fell off.

Just as I thought nothing worse could happen there were more shrieks from the WAAF Officers' Mess. Danny had followed us and, wearing my cap, he had climbed up on to the roof and tried unsuccessfully to remove a chimney-pot which had taken his fancy. Now he was sliding down the tiles, legs first, into the WAAF CO's bedroom window.

'Get down, get down, you dreadful boy!' Gloves screamed shrilly.

The other Norges, who were still fairly sober, scrambled up the drainpipe and retrieved both Danny and my cap. Gloves meanwhile, leaning out of the window, had spotted me minus cap and covered in blood, struggling in the arms of three Norwegian sailors. 'Report to me later, Wyndham!' she snarled. Hans, deep in gloom, had sunk on to a bench by the river and there he sat sobering up until one in the morning.

He kept telling me I was the girl he wanted to marry, he loved me passionately but he didn't think it would work because he's Norwegian and a regular sailor, and he couldn't see me living in Norway.

In spite of everything I realise I am still in love with him, much more than I am with Hamish – I love him so much that it hurts me to look at him, but I know he'll never marry me.

Monday

Feeling rather depressed after a terrible dressing-down from Gloves, I rang up Veronica and asked if I could come over and spend the day with her.

We had just finished lunch when a frantic orderly rings from the WAAF Mess to say that Hans is staging a sit-down strike in the ante-room and won't budge until he sees me! Great flap to catch the train, but worst of all I had just eaten lunch with fried onions.

Frantically chewed coffee and peppermint drops, and covered myself with Veronica's scent (My Sin, by Lanvin).

Hans was waiting in the ante-room. I gave him a big kiss, but he didn't even wince so all was well.

He was quite white with guilt and remorse, and couldn't remember a single thing that had happened the day before. He simply couldn't believe it when I told him, and said he had had a complete blackout. After that he became his old angelic self, and took me to the cinema – a thrilling Tarzan film with giant spiders and man-eating flowers – a real 2s. 9d. worth! He held me in a fierce clinch in the back seats.

He is still madly jealous about Hamish, which secretly pleases me.

Wednesday

One should never make the mistake of telling mother everything. My description of Hans getting drunk and sloshing me in the High Street brought an immediate horrified response. I wrote back as follows:

Darling Mama,

I think your idea about me inheriting my father's nature is a very dangerous one. It leads to the thought that I am fated to go to the dogs and can't escape it – so there's no use in trying and it's not really my fault. I know you think my father was a depraved rascal, and in many ways you are probably right. It's also true that I take after him, but there is absolutely no reason why hereditary vice shouldn't be overcome. And not by running away from it!

Until I met my father and went off drinking with him and until I met the Chelsea crowd and knew them and could laugh at them, I thought of it all as something glamorous, to be copied if possible. Now I've got to the stage where they don't mean a thing to me. In fact, their dirt and their uninhibited conversation tends, if anything, to bring out the prude in me through sheer bloody anti-suggestiveness! By the same token I suppose if I'd married someone madly 'county' and buried myself among horses and pheasants and things I should have hankered madly after Chelsea, investing it with spurious glamour and making myself thoroughly discontented.

Anyway, Hans is at heart a nice, clean, respectable chap — he's just not used to so much booze. By the way, I've had another weird letter from Petya, who is working like a demon, now that he knows he may be called up any minute. 'Beloved Thalia,' he writes, 'my guts are griped with mad enthusiasm!' (Who's Thalia, one of the Muses?)

I am amazed and impressed to hear that you are reading James Joyce! Are you really reading *Ulysses* or just the pornographic bits? Anyway I think it's frightfully brave of you.

Lots of love,
Joan

Saturday, 8th April

It has been a very short refit this time for Hans's and Danny's boats and the last day came all too soon. We were determined to crowd in as much as possible so made an early start on our bikes for the twelve-mile ride to Loch Ashie.

It was a wonderful day for early April, the sun shone out of a clear blue sky, but on the moors above Loch Ashie the grass was still white with frost. Ashie is a cold, ruffled grey lake, high above sea level, very desolate. As we whizzed along Hans recited 'Peer Gynt' and old Norwegian sagas at the top of his voice, and we chased a wildcat which vanished into the hills.

Then a long sweep down to two of the prettiest little lochs in Scotland, with green grass around them and birch trees, and lots of green hanging moss. We washed our faces and drank the ice-cold water, which was as smooth and bright as a steel mirror, with herons flapping away from it like little pterodactyls.

Had tea at Flichity Inn, sitting by the fire. Boiled eggs, hot baps with butter, homemade blackberry jam and fresh apple cakes, washed down by a big brown pot of tea, then home on my rattling old jalopy (service issue), a machine of great speed and insecurity.

The last six miles were downhill all the way, we flew down yelling and whooping, the sun and wind on our faces. I freewheeled with my hands off the handlebars and felt an incredible mixture of terror and excitement – rather like being very drunk. It was wonderful.

Later we collected a bottle of rum and climbed to the top of Inverness Castle. We could see the whole town spread out below us, enjoying itself on a Saturday night, and people dancing over the river where a man was playing a squeeze-box. The music came up to us most pleasantly – 'The Road to the Isles' and 'Will Ye No Come Back Again', while the sun set in a grey mist over the firth. I was happy to think that soon Hans and I would be dancing too, as we had an invitation to a thrash at a nearby 'drome.

I wore my white dress with the mothholes in it, very sexy, and just managed to put my hair up. Now that the Eton crop has grown out it is long enough to take a couple of combs.

It was a mixed dance of Fleet Air Arm and RAF, a very pukka affair with balloons and streamers and a cold buffet. Two pipers had been specially imported for the reels, and we could hear them coming from a long way off as they marched through the Mess, finally bursting into the ballroom at full blast with a drummer bringing up the rear.

Hans and I did a wildly improvised eightsome and an even wilder schottische – my suspender-belt bust in the middle of it (front suspenders only, thank God – so I carried gamely on, like a plane on one engine.).

About midnight I began to feel a bit tired so took two Benzedrine which kept me nicely sober in spite of gin, crème de menthe, rum and Algerian wine!

Finally the pipers started up a round waltz, a very slow dance to all the haunting old folk songs, ending up with 'Auld Lang Syne'. Hans and I danced as if we were one person – some nights it comes like that, and then dancing is mathematically controlled ecstasy. I leant my head against his shoulder and felt so happy I wanted to cry. There can be nothing in the world more romantic than to waltz slowly round a huge ballroom to 'Auld Lang Syne' played on the pipes – and to do it in the arms of someone you love!

We got a lift home with the band, me sitting on the saxophonist's knee, and they dropped us off at Ness Bank. From there we strolled down to the Islands and found an old summerhouse which is only used at weekends.

Hans pulled me down on to the dusty floor. We could hear a clock with a lame tick beating irregularly from behind a locked door. Hans's face, pale in the moonlight, as if underwater, with eyes like worn grey stones – so beautiful!

'My God, Joanie, it's so wonderful to be with you again,' he said. 'I'm so happy when I hold you in my arms like this.'

All the moodiness and harshness of earlier days had vanished and I realised that most of his bad temper had been simply because he was aching to go to bed with me again – how stupid of me not to have realised it earlier!

I took his seed in my mouth and drank it. It tasted strange like bitter almonds. Hans said it was the nicest thing anyone had ever done to him in his life.

Much later we staggered to our feet and dusted each other down, and Hans put on his operational Swedish raincoat – the one with the epaulettes that is pure Hollywood, and stood there smiling down at me with his cap stuck on the back of his head.

Tomorrow he goes back to the Shetlands and God knows when I shall see him again.

It must have been the Benzedrine because after he left I lay in bed and had hysterics and cried for hours – these pills definitely do stimulate your nerves! By the end of it I was so tired I could hardly even get into the bathroom to wash my face, but I couldn't sleep because my mind was still very active and kept sitting up and flapping its ears at me.

I tried reading Goethe and Baudelaire aloud but that didn't help so I took some sleeping tablets but they didn't work either. A rumba band from the night before kept romping through my head, and soon I was listening to the little birds singing as they got up and dressed, and a bloody great rook going ark-ark, and it was eight in the morning.

Now I feel simply dreadful and don't know how I shall ever make it to the Filter Room. As things turned out it was a piece of cake, just the odd reconnaissance plane snooping around. I felt fine, considering, and even managed to learn some new Norwegian verbs.

Thursday, 13th April

Pandora is still pining after her Canadian, but he has no intention of leaving his wife. She is by now one long skinny streak of misery, and I have had to sit over innumerable fish teas and listen to her moaning. I am not much better myself, moping as I am for the absent Hans. The couple of us are thinking of volunteering as living torpedoes.

We haunt the Cally, reviving old memories. We are also forced by boredom into seeing hundreds of bad flicks. I feel I know more about occupied Europe and the US Army Air Force than anyone else alive. Never again as long as I live do I want to see another pilot sink the entire Jap Navy with a few well-placed bombs. Never again do I want to see another heroic major or schoolmaster or female guerilla, or a fat Gestapo villain eating chocolates and smoking through a long holder while he says, 'We have ways of making you talk.' Oscar, on the other hand, seems to have gone off Danny. He is really too mad for a girl to take seriously.

Hamish writes that he is still rotting in a staff job in London, but hopes to get posted soon. The only cheerful news concerns Veronica. Two days ago a Czech pilot thumbed a lift from her way up in the wilds. She happened to mention her husband's name and lo and behold this chap had found him in a field with two ribs broken, dressed him as a peasant woman and taken him to the nearest village where he was given a blood transfusion and hidden by the peasants. The Czech escaped six weeks later but left Alan completely recovered with the other guerillas in the mountains.

Friday, 28th April

Veronica and I had a hysterical lunch today, dancing and embracing in the middle of the High Street and celebrated by going into the town's only smart hat shop and buying something ridiculous with feathers on it.

5th May

I think spring has definitely come – there's a warm, nutty smell of gorse on the wind, and bluebells, violets and primroses are out.

We get plenty of fresh salmon, now that the snow-water is coming down from the mountains, and the Ness is swollen, full of fish rushing off to spawn. Today half the town was leaning on the railings outside our front porch watching a little man land a huge salmon with all the colours of the rainbow on its side.

I am beginning to feel a bit more cheerful, what with Hans's letters arriving regularly. Another exciting arrival has been my contact lenses! At first they were very uncomfortable and I was constantly afraid they would disappear into the back of my head and never be seen again, but I am beginning to get used to them.

Last night I tried them out at a film party in the RAF Mess. The film was *Casablanca* with Ingrid Bergman and we watched it from armchairs, full of gin, and danced afterwards. As everybody sees in me a purely spurious resemblance to Ingrid B, my success was assured, especially without the goggles.

The CO told me I had the most amazing eyes, and so I should have, with my slight squint magnified by two enormous glass goldfish bowls. Later we danced to 'As Time Goes By' and he breathed 'You are adorable' heavily into my ear – so I think the £25 was money well spent. I only wish Hans was here to be impressed.

His last letter was very sweet, and filled me with guilt for not having written. It is typed on an official signals form:

To: The dear little beautiful kind Joan.
From: The big bad ugly Hansemann.
Date: 1st May 1944.
Ref: No letter from you in a long, long time.

He bemoans that I have left a poor refugee alone in a strange country with no one to care for him, and ends, 'I should damned much like to see you again – it would be too terrible if you had totally forgotten me.' I practically burst into tears, and wrote to him right away enclosing a photo. If only I could get up to Shetland to see him.

Monday, 5th June

Enormous excitement! Last night the Fifth Army entered Rome – all sorts of crazy rumours are going the rounds. I'm on night watch and there is tremendous activity, our carriers and gliders have landed behind the German defences in Normandy. Thousands of bombers are crossing the French coast.

We came off night watch at 9.30 a.m. and switched on the radio, just as they were sounding the alert to the various countries. Of course we roused the whole house and everyone came in and sat around the wireless to hear it. It really was terrifically exciting, D–Day at last!

Friday, 9th June

Saw the latest newsreels of the Armada, and the gliders going in. They are marvellous.

Saturday, 10th June

Veronica and I are gloating over the stories about Shimi. His commandos refused to wear helmets and went into the attack in their green berets, with Piper William Millin leading the way.

'Give us "Highland Laddie" man!' Shimi yelled as he plunged into the sea up to his armpits.

Once on shore the piper paraded up and down the beach playing 'Road to the Isles', oblivious of the shells and shouts of 'get down you silly bugger!' Relieving the bridge over the river Orme, he strolled along it in his plimsolls, as if he were inspecting a herd of bulls, with his inevitable pipers – who, I think, really deserve a medal – playing 'Blue Bonnets over the Border'.

The Scottish papers gave him a colossal spread on the lines of 'Tall handsome Lord Lovat, a leader any man would die for, strolled up to the bridgehead in an open-neck pullover, a piper on either side of him' and so on. Veronica and I, of course, are lapping it up. It even consoles her for the awful fact that she has got piles!

Wednesday, 14th June

Huge family flap amongst the Lovats as Shimi has got a lump of shrapnel in his stomach. He was shot at a farmhouse near Saulnier, and his wounds are too extensive even to be sewn up. But he is not expected to die, thank God.

Hamish, who was not sent over after all on D-Day, takes it all a bit sourly. It must be quite maddening to see pictures of your cousin, pale and interesting in satin pyjamas, extending a limp hand to the Queen on the front page of the *Daily Express*, while you have been stuck in England and missed all the fun.

Veronica's Czech still swears that he has seen her husband alive. He is a complete adventurer but seems honest. Lady Lovat, however, is still unconvinced and says that if he is lying she will tear him limb from limb. But the stories he told! Specially about Orianberg concentration camp – every time I hear about these camps I go cold all over. In the evening I washed Veronica's hair and drew nursery-rhyme pictures for the children.

Ever since the invasion we have been working on a three-watch basis, which is frightfully hard, with very little sleep and no days off at all. The twenty-four hours are split into three eight-hour stretches and we do a different one every day or night, with eight hours' rest. Nevertheless, Oscar, Pandora and I are all on watch together and we have such fun, and giggle so hysterically that we really don't care. Also, Zoe Hicks's boyfriend is the controller so he lets us do what we like on watch.

Poor Pandora, as well as suffering from unrequited love, has toothache, spots and suspected gallstones. She appears to be on the point of physically disintegrating altogether. In fact, we are all pretty tired and run down. A strange new type of bomb landed in the south last week. Apparently it comes over on its own, without an aircraft, and you know it's going to drop when you hear the engine cut out.

Friday, 7th July

Flying bombs on London now by day and night. My mother didn't want me to come on leave, but I came anyhow, because I hoped Hamish might ring up before he was posted overseas.

The devastation is dreadful, so many familiar places ruined and blackened. Ma is on night watch at Dovehouse Street, so I go along to help out. There are lots of casualties.

By Thursday there was a lull, so we used a whole week's meat ration on shepherd's pie, played mah-jong, and listened to Mama's favourite record, Barbara Mullen singing 'Jeanie with the Light Brown Hair'. Halfway through the meal Hamish finally rang up, and I went weak at the knees, yet again.

He wants to see me on Saturday (which is my last day) and take me to a very grand party given by some 'cousins' of mine called Egremont. It seems weird and incongruous that people are still giving parties with all this devastation going on, but it seems they do.

It was on the first floor of a beautiful Regency house and I went with high expectations, looking v. glamorous in pale blue. As Hamish had told me Lord Egremont was a sort of relation of mine I expected at least an 'Oh, hello, you must be cousin Joan,' but not a sausage. Lord E took my hand briefly and looked straight through me. Perhaps I was the wrong sort of Wyndham.

His wife kept darting forward to meet her guests with cries of 'Darling!', pursing her mouth an inch away from their cheeks and making a little humming sound which sounded like 'mm, bless you!'

I was introduced to people who didn't want to speak to me, some of them extending their hands sideways like flippers without even stopping their conversations. Others, less lucky, were actually trapped into talking to me, their eyes looking wildly over my shoulder in search of succour. In the slightest pause, they would rush off to the bar and never come back.

Hamish, the shit, was chatting up a gorgeous young Argentinian heiress, wearing the smartest black dress I had ever seen, and dripping with what were obviously real emeralds. He ignored me completely, not dancing with me once. I think I would have died if it hadn't been for a wonderful red-haired Canadian. Being a Canadian he obviously didn't know that I was the wrong sort of Wyndham and couldn't get over his luck at getting me.

We jitterbugged wildly, he threw me in the air and whirled me round his head. We were certainly the best dancers there. Most of the 'gels' danced extraordinarily badly, prancing coltishly in a rather disjointed way as if they thought it bad form to know the steps.

Every time I looked round I could see Hamish doing wild fandangoes with his new 'flirt'. I felt sick with misery and rejection.

At about one in the morning, strange tribal rites began to take place, much to the astonishment of my Canadian.

There was a game called Pyramids where everybody climbs on top of each other in the middle of the dancefloor until the entire teetering mound collapses in a heap of crumpled satin and wildly waving legs in laddered silk stockings. Jewelled earrings flew skidding across the floor, and an impassive footman collected them in a white silk handkerchief, and handed them to one of the duchesses who were sitting round the edge of the floor on little gilt chairs.

Then the men started something called cock fighting, riding each other's shoulders and tearing each other's fine white shirts to rags.

'Gee!' was all the Canadian could say.

Sadly enough he had to leave to catch his transport, so as Hamish was still galumphing around with his bloody Argentinian, I decided to behave badly too, got off with a nice dark man called Maurice Macmillan and snogged with him in the back of his car in the square. Unfortunately his wife caught us so I decided to take a taxi home. It really hadn't been my night. I don't think I really fit in with these very smart people.

Next day Hamish rang up to apologise, but it was too late – my leave was over.

Later he wrote: 'Miserere, mea culpa! I know I behaved like a shit and a bounder. Please, please forgive me.'

So of course I did.

Thursday, 20th July

An attack on Hitler's life, but unfortunately the bastard wasn't killed.

We are having a bit of a lull on watch at the moment so I'm getting on with my Norwegian, studying from a book called *Norwegian in Three Months without a Tutor*. It is very simple, a child could learn it – all the verb endings are the same. You say 'I love, he love, you love' and so on, and if you want to put it in the past you just add on 'et'. Now Hans and I can write to each other in Norwegian.

Sometimes Pandora and I have long discussions about God (she also being a Catholic), and we have come up with some very strange definitions for Him. For instance:

1. He is an enormous peppermint humbug, striped in black and white, for good and evil (the Manichean theory).

2. He is like a huge sunlamp – if you rub on enough of the oil of virtue during your lifetime, you bask in His warmth when you die and go a beautiful brown! If, on the other hand, you have neglected to use the oil, you fry! (This does away with any need for the theory of heaven and hell.)

3. He is a football player, all-powerful, with the ball at His feet, and not another player on the field – this soon gets boring, so He invents the devil to have someone who can kick the ball back at Him.

Thoughts like these would never have occurred to me some years ago – I think all the horrors of war have been slowly eroding my belief in an all-good and all-powerful God.

Friday, 25th August

Darling Mama,

This is rather a bad moment to write to you. Paris has just been liberated and I've discovered myself to be in love with Hamish after all! I feel sick, flat on my back with nervous migraine and an awful desire to throw up. He rang me up and in two days' time he goes to France. I keep thinking I've got over him, and then I hear his voice and I'm a 'goner' again, in spite of his flirtation with the Argentinian lady, and his letters which say, 'Please don't worry about me, I am just a shit and a pretty useless sort of bastard, blessed with a certain amount of spurious charm, etc.' He is obviously determined to be a bounder and I am in an awful state of gloom.

He is shortly going off to Belgium to ~~train guerillas who are going to be parachuted into France~~ Sorry, I wasn't supposed to tell you that, but all I can say is that it's something to do with '*being dropped*'!

Veronica practically weeps over me as she has set her heart on making a match between us. I beg her not to say anything to Hamish in case he gets that trapped feeling, so she contents herself with telling him at frequent intervals that all South American women grow long black beards after fifty.

Please will you and Sid make a novena to the Sacred Heart that he'll want to settle down after the war and marry me? It would be wonderful but somehow I haven't much hope. I don't know what is wrong with me but somehow I always seem to be crazy about some man who doesn't want to marry me!

Hans writes wonderfully passionate letters, but I think it's only because he's so bored and frustrated in Shetland. He too is dead set against matrimony!

Please could you send me a good stiff hairbrush with black bristles, the kind that practically scalps you every time you use it? Also, if you can manage it, I'd like a subscription to *Horizon* and one to Boots library – 7/6d. a quarter – and also some Chivers jellies (raspberry if poss.).

Many thanks for the fruit cake, but it was in the sort of tin that only dynamite can open. I wrestled with it for two days, maddened with hunger and dripping with blood, having broken two knives on it. Finally, covered in sticking-plaster and in black despair, I took it to the kitchen where they hacked it open with an axe. It was excellent, thanks most awfully, and luckily I ate most of it before the love-bug laid me low.

12th September 1944

Brussels has been liberated, and Hamish is there on very secret work. He says he is scared stiff. As for me, my heart, which was obviously bruised but not broken, is slowly mending. I have decided to give up men and lead a quiet life. For instance, Oscar and I now go to cookery classes! Last week we made a wonderful batch of gingerbread and lived on it for the whole week. Also classes in Scottish Highland dancing. Most exhausting and therapeutic. I am also knitting a scarf, which is made from Air Force wool – the consistency of old tarry rope, the finished result being like a piece of corrugated iron!

We have this Norwegian Air Force boy, Reidar, on watch with us – he is short and rather plain, with glasses, but very athletic. He teaches me Norwegian grammar, and I'm teaching him to knit! I am also doing my best to turn him into a pounce-proof, platonic, cycling companion, so on the first sunny day we had, I decided to try him out on the twenty-five miles from Beauly to Eskerdale.

After a couple of miles there was a diversion.

'Aha!' he exclaims. 'Ein liten pinsvin,' which translated literally means 'a little prickle pig'. The hedgehog had a very winning little face, but smelt abominable. We sat and played with it for a bit but then I could see a certain look on Reidar's face and he took his glasses off – always a bad sign – so held the 'pinsvin' firmly in my lap like a living chastity belt. However, it takes more than a hedgehog to deter a Norwegian and before I knew what was happening – hey presto! – there I was flat on my back. Very damp it was too.

After half an hour of fruitless struggle Rei must have decided to work it off some other way, for to my amazement he suddenly leapt to his feet and disappeared round a clump of trees at a steady canter.

I took the opportunity of going behind a bush to pee, and when I peered round the foliage there he was rounding the corner for the second time, arms going like pistons, knees up to his chin, and a look of firm endeavour in his eyes as he thundered past to disappear once more into the distance.

Finally, after a third lap, he came panting up to me, took my head under his arm and before you could say knife had hurled me over his shoulder in a forward somersault.

'Ah, now I feel much better!' he said with satisfaction – which was more than I did. By now I had come to the conclusion that safety lay in never getting off my bike at all, even for the hills. Since then, thank God, he seems to have developed a protective instinct towards me and he feels sure I must have been his sister or mother in a previous incarnation!

A strange letter arrives from Hans – I had written to him about Reidar and how I was repelling his advances. I thought it might amuse and reassure him – not at all!

'*Never* write me such things again, I do not wish to hear them! Can you not imagine what this poor chap suffers under such a circumstance? There is a name in Norway for girls who treat men so!' He was really furious – I was flabbergasted.

Hamish writes from Brussels that he is still a bit scared but is now having fun with the Maquis.

10th October

The first V2s landed on London. They are like rockets, and are even worse than the doodlebugs.

11th October

My twenty-third birthday. Reidar has invited me for dinner at the Cally, followed by a dance – what he describes as 'a hot night out'. Off I went, putting my faith in God and a strong pair of lock-knit Directoire knickers.

We danced to Harry Perry and his Radio Rhythm Club which is a really hot band from London. Reidar and I went to town in a big way and cut quite a rug. Reidar was hep and I was pretty solid myself, so you can imagine we were both well in the groove.

Another letter from Hamish in Brussels. He is enjoying the war hugely now, but says that the guerillas – apart from a few fine types – are a rather smelly and furtive lot and there are no attractive women, which I am glad of. He also sent me an enormous bottle of Chanel No. 5 for my birthday, enough to float a battleship, which has made me the envy of my mates!

I hadn't heard from Hans for ages, but suddenly got a wire the other day which just said 'FORTY INCHES, MY SWEET LOVE'. I couldn't think what the hell he meant until I remembered I'd asked him his chest measurements for a pullover for Christmas, which I'm going to knit.

Poor Danny is in hospital with shrapnel in his leg, so Hans has command of the flotilla.

Christmas 1944

The whole Mess was decorated with candles, pine branches and artificial snow. It was a beautiful clear day. Reidar gave me a pale blue Shetland shawl, thin as a spider's web, which I wore over my hair for dinner at the Cally.

We were on watch all Xmas night, dancing to the gramophone, throwing turkey bones down from the gallery, and nothing on the map but a large sausage with horns, labelled 'Hostile'. The Controller was made to sweep the floor and the plotters did the controlling. We painted an indelible beard and moustache on the CO while he was asleep.

About 7 a.m. the men's watch came on roaring drunk, headed by the flight sergeant in a top hat and artificial black whiskers. He bowed low to me and said, 'Good morning, Reverend Mother!' before staggering to his post on the table. Luckily it was a quiet night.

Afterwards everyone came down to the WAAF Officers' Mess and we started all over again. I took two Benzedrine, removed my shoes and danced in my bedsocks.

Reidar was doing some serious drinking with a very ropy flying type called Wing-Commander Carruthers. When the booze finally ran out they raided the bathroom and found a bottle of Gloves's cough mixture (containing alcohol) which they drained to the dregs.

After this they progressed from the patriotic – 'Up King Olaf! Sorry old chap, I mean Haakon!' – to the sentimental – 'I love this woman, she is fine Nordic type,' 'Piece of cake, bang on!' Then Rei uttered his famous last words, 'Watch me walk along this straight line,' and fell like a stone. As I tried to lift him he cried, 'Leave me alone! This is a world of men!' and passed out again.

Searching in the Mess for someone to give me a hand I came across Pandora and Oscar inextricably entangled with five bomber boys from Tain. They sprang apart – I hastily turned off the light and withdrew.

At 6.30 a.m., an unexpected and extremely welcome arrival of transport. They removed two unconscious men and laid them tenderly on the back seat.

After that we all ate macaroni cheese and prunes and went to bed for the day.

Boxing Day

As soon as I had sobered up sufficiently, I wrote Mama a letter.

Darling Mama,

By this time Xmas will be over so I can only hope it was as happy for you as the V2s permitted. Anyway, I hope the gin and Benzedrine helped a little towards the festive spirit – did they arrive in time?

We had a wizard time on watch, with everybody very drunk and happy, and a crazy feeling that perhaps this would be our last wartime Christmas. Everything is going so well on the second front, what with the Yanks holding out against von

Runstedt, and the Russians reaching the Danube.

A letter has arrived from Petya – 'Oh curse, oh damn, no white, no ochre, no varnish, no mastic, no dinner, no coal, no light, oh curse and damn! I try very hard to pull myself together.' It doesn't sound as if *he* can have had a very happy Christmas, but at least he hasn't been called up yet.

Thank you very much for your Christmas books. I quite like some of Edith Sitwell, but she does go on a bit, doesn't she? I mean, if she cut everything by half and didn't repeat her ideas and adjectives so much she wouldn't be half bad.

Also thanks for the book about the two Saint Teresas – what hell Carmel must have been for those poor nuns! Imagine, no heating! As for Thérèse of Lisieux's 'Little Sayings', they still irritate me profoundly but I think Teresa of Avila must have been a terrific woman.

I've bought a dress with your £2 to wear for our New Year's party. It was the nicest and most unpractical thing I could think of, a kind of pale blue watered silk, extremely smart and only £2 13s.

If you are forwarding my trunk, you could put a few things in it. Not my tin hat, but my purple Jaeger jacket with the zip, the nigger-brown coat and skirt from B & H, my white detachable lace collar which is somewhere, filthy dirty, and a pair of patterned lisle stockings. Also, if you can find them, a pot of Ida Hahn matt foundation cream (green lid), my eyelash curlers and Frazer's *Golden Bough* – I think that's about all!

Love,

Joan

New Year was the last good time we all had together before the blow fell. I wore my new blue dress to the party and there was a huge cold buffet but I was too excited to eat. When midnight sounded we cheered every stroke and sang 'Auld Lang Syne', and I was kissed by almost every man in the Mess – as there were about one hundred-odd pilots it was a bit of a do! The band was terrific and the men were queueing up to dance – lovely! Reidar and I were really in the groove.

In the morning the tannoy woke us at 6.30, roaring away through the camp that it was 1st January 1945 and a fine, clear morning.

Saturday, 6th January

Five days later the blow fell. I was summoned to the CO's office. He was looking embarrassed and fingering a piece of paper.

'I'm afraid I have some rather bad news for you, Wyndham,' he said, not looking up at me at all. 'I have a posting for you here – it's to Watnall, effective from January 25th.'

He went on to give further details, but then broke off, aware that I was crying unashamedly. I felt as a woman would if she were suddenly told she must leave her husband, her children and her home and go and live in darkest Africa. The CO was very sympathetic, but he told me there was nothing he could do. I bet it was that bitch Gloves – may she rot in hell!

Oscar and I have been crying solidly for two days and she is trying to get a posting too. My only comfort is that Pandora is going with me. I don't know much about Watnall except that it's in a coal-mining area somewhere near Nottingham, a rather ugly and dismal place.

Two days later

I have just about managed to pull myself together. There is so much to do now – not just to say goodbye to Inverness, but also to try to get a flight out to the Shetlands and see Hans for one last time. I rang up Longman's Airfield and they said there was a naval plane going up there on Friday, so I booked a seat on it.

After that we went to a dance at the Cally, had haggis and whisky and danced the last eightsome reel and the last waltz. It was a slow waltz and very appropriate too, with Loch Lomond and never meeting again and taking the high road, etc.

Friday, 12th

Up early to catch the naval plane from Longman's. The sun was just rising as the plane took off into a clear blue sky – the whole of Scotland was under snow. Every colour in the rainbow lay in bands across the horizon, from yellow and green and turquoise blue to violet and rose, the mountains behind white and dazzling with snow, almost iridescent, and the sun red like fire. All these colours were reflected in the glass-smooth waters of the firth. It was one of the most beautiful things I ever saw in my life, quite unbelievable.

Soon we could see the red cliffs of Orkney crowned with their clouds of sea birds – here the snow stopped as though a line had been drawn, and the Shetland Isles lay ahead.

I had dreamt about them for so long they had become unreal to me. I had imagined huge whales that blew off with a noise like thunder, seals on pink granite rocks, and blond, bony Shetlanders cutting peat. I had dreamt of the *aurora borealis*, and the sun going down at midnight to rise again at 2 a.m. in the same red clouds that it had set in, and rock eagles nesting in the pink cliffs of Papa Stour.

I knew instinctively that the islands would be nothing like this, just as I knew that Hans's boat might not be there – it could be out on a raid or on manoeuvres – but I kept my fingers crossed.

We landed at Sumburgh in a wind that cut like a knife, and found a naval car waiting to take us into Lerwick. Now my heart was pounding wildly – because in a few minutes I'd know my fate. We reached the fish quay, and there, like a miracle, was Hans's boat anchored within a few feet of me. I hailed a Norwegian sailor who was patrolling with a pistol in his belt.

'Please tell the captain there is someone to see him,' I said. He grinned from ear to ear and vanished below. After a few minutes he returned with my beautiful Hansemann who leapt on shore wearing sea boots and a very tasty affair known as a bridge coat, which made him look like a barrel of rum.

For one moment I thought he was taken aback at seeing me, but then a big smile spread across his face, and he hugged me hard while the little sailor looked the other way.

He seems thinner and more nervous and smokes like a chimney, but otherwise just the same and looks about nineteen.

'What a lovely surprise, Joanie,' he said. 'I suppose we'd better get you fixed up with a room at the Queen's Hotel.'

You? I wondered. Why not us? Of course they are very moral up here, but couldn't I pretend to be his wife, like at Drumnadrochit?

Apparently not. Hans firmly ordered a single room.

'You know I'm a big man now,' he went on, 'CO of the flotilla, so I have a lot of stuff to see to this afternoon – but if you come to the boat about six I will organise a big party.' I was left alone in the freezing lounge of the hotel feeling a bit let down. Two stuffed birds that appeared to be albatrosses and a picture of 'Lord Kitchener's Return' stared back at me. Wasn't there heating anywhere?

Finally I persuaded the dour proprietress to light me a tiny fire in my bedroom, which resembled an igloo. Miserably I crouched over the embers in my greatcoat. Later I plucked up enough courage to brave the bathroom down the corridor, and found the water quite warm but dark peaty-brown like bathing in hot whisky.

Meanwhile Hans had hoisted the gin pennant, and sent signals to all the rest of the flotilla. 'Request pleasure ship's company immediately. Joan from Inverness is here.' Back came the answers – 'Very many pleasures.' 'Very nice thank you.' 'Allow twenty minutes for taking off beard.'

Watching Hans with his shipmates I thought how they were far more loving and united than any family. Kurt, the No. 1, calls Hans 'Fader', he is 'Onkel', and the little midshipman is 'Sonn'. It is a small, closed world, with its own slang and its own deep loyalties, and I couldn't help feeling a bit left out, though they were very kind and gave me their sweet coupons.

Danny is still in hospital with shrapnel in his leg – they think he may lose it. They were operating up north, lying in wait for a German convoy, when their boat was sunk by enemy aircraft, and Danny was wounded. They nearly drowned but managed to reach a barren island where they lived for a week, helping the islanders with their cooking and net-mending, and placating them with large tins of Spam. Hans lost everything, including his precious Dunhill pipe, and now they have a new boat.

They miss Danny terribly and there were sad reminiscences like, 'Do you remember the night when we found him on the quayside in his pyjamas trying to chew through an electric cable with his teeth?' Or, 'How about when he filled his sea boots with water and waved them under the padre's nose chanting "Change the water into wine!"'

Soon the flotilla began to roll in, some sober, some slightly whizzed, some gloriously and homerically stinkers. Everyone was delighted to see me again. There were guitars and accordions so we sang sea shanties, then everything from 'Loch Lomond' to 'Lili Marlene'. There were men lying on the floor, heaped up on bunks, dancing on the table. It was a grand party, and Hans, who was wearing my earrings, got happily drunk, but almost made a point of not showing me any special affection. I imagined he was shy in front of his new crew.

Then to my surprise, a little Norwegian Wren appeared.

'Who's that?' I asked suspiciously.

'Oh,' Hans said casually, 'that's Lieven, she's a mother to us all.'

Lucky old Lieven, I thought, wondering how many of the men there had been her lovers. She certainly didn't look the motherly type.

Hans saw me to the hotel at one o'clock, but didn't suggest coming in. From the quayside I could hear raucous voices raised in the flotilla song:

> Death to the Germans, they took our land from us,
> Ready with the guns, ready with the torpedoes. . . .

How I longed to be back there, in the warm, crowded wardroom, singing along with them, one of the boys.

I watched Hans's figure dwindling into the mist. Never in my life have I wanted so much to be a man.

Slept, fully dressed, between sheets that crackled with the cold.

Saturday, 13th January

Woke at lunchtime and looked out of the window straight down to the water. A sailor was skipping in the pale sunshine. Boats were coming and going and gun crews were whirling round in their turrets dressed like mediaeval pirates. In front of the boats was parked a naval car and in it sat Hans waiting to take me on a tour of Shetland.

It is a fascinating country, no trees, just peat and rock, nothing but outlines, and the beautiful shapes of the little islands. Being without decoration it depends on the light for its quality of magic. The peasants knit delicate lacy shawls, and the walls of their cottages are bright with pink, green and yellow sheepskins pegged out to dry. They speak a curious language, half English and half Norse.

Hoping to buy fresh eggs, we knocked on the door of a stone farmhouse.

A woman opened the door dressed like Peer Gynt's mother in a pointed cap of sealskin edged with rabbit fur, and with two long thongs hanging down in front. Her skirts were down to her feet and her face was the colour of the peat-stack outside her cottage. She asked us in and the smell of the living room nearly made us pass out. We got our eggs and headed for home – and still Hans hadn't kissed me.

Sunday, 14th January

My last night and my last chance of sleeping with Hans. How we would have longed for a room like this in the old days, when we wandered the Islands and lay on damp grass.

Feeling like a cheap tart I put on civvies and rather overdid the make-up.

He finally turned up with a huge chap who eats ties at parties called Stefan the Tie-eater. To my dismay they suggested we spend the evening at Lieven's flat.

She had lit candles and was handing round plates of nuts and raisins, looking quite alarmingly pretty in a tweed skirt and red jumper. She put on a record of Norwegian folk music and danced with Hans. Clasped to the massive chest of Tie-eater I watched with jealous rage as they hopped and skipped round the room. Then he pulled her to him and began to dance more closely. I decided to get very drunk.

A couple of hours later, once more confronted by stuffed birds and 'Kitchener's Return', I lost all sense of pride and simply grabbed Hans by the arm as he turned to leave.

'Hans – why don't you stay with me? Don't you want to sleep with me?'

He looked dreadfully embarrassed. 'You know I really love you, Joanie,' he said finally, 'You're the best comrade I ever had. I just don't want to spoil our relationship and make it sordid. It's so good the way it is.'

'What do you mean, spoil?'

'Well, when I sleep with you I feel a real shit, knowing all the time that you want to marry me, and knowing that I can't. I never would, darling – you see I just couldn't stand the responsibility. It would drive me mad.'

'But it doesn't matter,' I said desperately. 'I don't mind if you don't marry me, I just want to be with you now.'

Hans, if possible, looked even more embarrassed. 'There is something else,' he said, 'something that I find very difficult to say to you. You see, when I make love to you I don't feel that you really like it – at least not the way some women like it. And you've no idea what that does to a man.'

Not like it! When I think of all the times I've lavished tenderness and caresses on him and all the joy that I've taken in his kisses and it had all been meaningless to him just because I didn't have an orgasm!

It occurred to me in a flash that he had been having Lieven and that she was probably sexy as hell. I shook with rage and began to cry. Hans took me in his arms and kissed me and comforted me. He told me I was the only woman he had ever really loved, that he loves me like he does his mates. I suppose that means he thinks of me as a man (in his eyes, the highest compliment), and I suppose I ought to feel flattered. But I don't.

Suddenly he cried, 'I am the worst man in the world!' and hurtled out of the conservatory doors, and there I was, alone again with those bloody birds.

Thursday, 18th January

My last day. I woke early feeling stiff with cold and terribly depressed. I stood at the window and watched the light begin to grow, and men coming out yawning and stretching to begin their work on the guns. The sailor with the skipping rope came on deck in the half light, spat into the sea, took out his rope and began a slow, graceful workout down the quayside.

Quickly I got dressed and ran down to where Hans's boat was moored. A horrified steward told me that the chief never rose before eleven. Nevertheless I pushed past him, and went below to wake Onkel, Fader and Sonn. Tie-eater was lying on the floor fully clothed, snoring heavily. The 'Chief' was snoozing like a baby in blue navy-issue pyjamas, his hair rumpled like that of a newly hatched chick. I woke him with a kiss and we all had breakfast together, bacon, eggs and beer. Time was running out, and soon I had to say goodbye to this little family. When it came to Hans's turn he acted very tough and I endeavoured to do the same. It was a very good show.

I left him in the Ops room being briefed and Tie-eater drove me to Sumburgh with a crate of beer in the back of the car. We arrived pretty whizzed, had more drinks in the Mess and finally staggered on to the frozen runway singing the flotilla song, where I was hauled aboard the naval plane by four strong arms.

There was a gale blowing, so strong you could hardly stand, and some doubt as to whether we would take off, but alas we did – I have never felt so awful, or been so ill! For three hours I didn't open my eyes, hunched miserably over a large paper bag, as the little aircraft tossed, lurched and bumped like a mad thing. I even prayed for it to plunge straight into the North Sea!

When we finally reached Inverness, I reeled into the Station Hotel more dead than alive, and a kind waitress brought me coffee and aspirin.

Only then did it really hit me that I would probably never see Hans again.

BOOK IV

Sunday, 28th January 1945

WATNALL, NOTTINGHAMSHIRE

Darling Mama,

You must not worry any more about those nasty old flying bombs as I am now personally responsible for stopping them from reaching you! We have the launching pads quite near the area of our plotting table, and bags of panic when they start coming over.

Did you know that Mark XIV Spits and Hawker Tempests can catch a doodlebug when it's flying low and blow it up? Sometimes they even knock it out of the sky with their wings, and send it into the sea! Unfortunately there doesn't seem to be much we can do against the V2 rockets.

The work here is basically the same as in Scotland, but more exciting. We actually feel we are doing something worthwhile, especially if I can stop the doodles from reaching you.

Nevertheless, I'm still furious about my move and miserable in this hideous industrial town, away from all my friends and with nothing but ugliness to see wherever I look. I keep thinking of those gorgeous days on Shetland, like a particularly thrilling dream. Hans, I know, really loved to see me up there, and so it was worthwhile being so sick on the way back.

It's sad in a way that he doesn't want to get married but frankly I'd just as soon be his friend, perhaps more so. I don't think I would ever have really fitted in in Norway, staggering myopically around and falling off my skis, and saying 'fy faen' in front of his mother.

As it is I feel proud to be accepted by him and his mates as a good chap, in spite of being a girl. When I hear them talking I sometimes wish to God I wasn't a woman – such friendship and loyalty and such unabashed patriotism! It is a change to be with people who are not embarrassed by loving their country and don't mind admitting that they hate the Germans and are proud of their flotilla.

Pandora is here, Oscar has applied for a transfer, but in the meantime I am shacked up with old Gussy – my mate from Preston – in a miner's cottage. Plenty of coal for the fires and a black rim around the bath. The couple are called Owen, hordes of children – even the baby howls in Welsh. Father is dark, haggard and handsome, and listens to festival choirs on the radio. Mother has lost nearly all her teeth. She sings wild Penillions (like in Mary Webb) spitting madly through her remaining stumps.

Tonight is Sunday, so I can hear them below us singing 'Jerusalem' in close harmony. Now it's changed to 'Those in Peril on the Sea', father booming in with a bass descant.

Gussy is still as tarty as ever and is having an affair with the CO of our station! At the moment she is having her usual monthly flap over the delays of nature and taking awful pink pills which give her diarrhoea. She has lent my Henry Miller to the CO, who lent it to the Adjutant and now it's gone right round the camp so everybody thinks I am a 'bad type'. I've found some very funny rude bits in Chaucer's 'Miller's Tale' – will send them to you next time.

Now they're on to 'Aberystwyth' – not much sleep tonight I fear.

No more news except that Gussy is trying to persuade me to 'brighten' my hair with Hiltone, so if I come home a platinum blonde you will know that 'me 'and slipped'!

Love,
Joan

February 1945

Ugly and squalid Watnall may be, but unlike all the other places I've been stationed at so far, it has one great advantage – a mixed Mess! There is a big manor house for the men and huts in the surrounding ground for us WAAFs. At the moment they haven't got a vacancy, so I am still stuck, with Gussy, in a temporary billet.

Pandora – lucky blighter – has already gone on to the mixed Mess, and she says it is fabulous! So we sit in our horrid room, eating chockies given to Gussy by the CO (her lover), and dream of this palace of delights that looms on the horizon.

Gussy has, if possible, got even sexier since I saw her last in Preston. She tells me that now she can have an orgasm just by leaning over the rail of the Filter Room balcony and rubbing herself against it. To make things even better she puts lots of starch into her shirts and doesn't wear a bra.

I told her about Dr Schliemann and she found it terribly funny. She thinks we've been taken for a ride and all we really needed was the right man. I asked her if the CO was OK and she said, 'Oh he's fine, except that he will chase me round the room on all fours barking like a dog.'

Friday, 16th February

The great day has finally arrived, and we are moving into Buxton Hall. There is something incredibly exciting and stimulating about a mixed Mess, designed as it is to give us maximum opportunity for meeting the opposite sex. The only snag is you have to try and look attractive all the time and can't stroll around with no make-up and pipe-cleaners in your hair.

Apart from our sleeping quarters, there is a big communal dining room, an ante-room, and off this the bar – full of wrecked and randy fighter types, either grounded or resting between missions.

I wandered in there alone on my first night, feeling incredibly nervous and excited, and wearing my contact lenses. I find that now I have left off my glasses lots of men mistake my astigmatism for the wild and roving glance of passion. One or two people have told me I look ready for anything, which of course is not true at all!

I sat down in a corner with my drink and looked around. Half the bar seemed to be talking about the raid on Dresden two nights ago, which they seem to consider a 'jolly good show'. I feel quite horrified at the thought of all those innocent people being killed – no matter what the Germans did to London and Coventry. But it wouldn't do to voice such opinions here; the feeling for revenge is very strong. Another rather jolly group were inventing rude definitions for the various parts of an aeroplane, e.g. What is a ball-race? Answer: A cat with ten yards start on the vet.

Gussy joined us and in no time at all we were being offered G & Ts. I have never known people to be so nice and friendly to a 'new girl'. I realised that although I had been in the WAAF for nearly four years, it was the first time I'd ever had the chance to meet and live with fighter pilots. They are really a race apart, tough, crazy and cynical, but also intelligent and very funny. There was one pilot who seemed different from the rest, a very suave Pole with white eyelashes, platinum hair, huge padded shoulders and narrow hips.

'Watch out for that type,' Gussy said, 'he's one of those Poles who can kiss your hand and throw you on to a bed in one consecutive movement.' After he had eyed us up for a bit he slunk over, swinging his hips in a very sexy way, and asked if we'd like a drink, which we readily agreed to.

'What's your name?' I asked, flapping the old eyelashes at him.

'Wladzimierz!' he replied tersely, putting me off my stroke a bit, 'but you can call me Vlady.'

Apparently he is the youngest squadron leader in the Polish Air Force, over here from France on six months' rest. He has the DSO, DFC with two bars and the Polish VC. According to Gussy, no WAAF has ever been known to resist him, but funnily enough I didn't find him at all attractive – he was too obviously aware of his wolf-like charms. However, he took quite a fancy to me, ignoring Gussy, and giving me long meaningful looks from his ice-cold green eyes.

Luckily the dinner gong sounded, and we all surged into the Mess Hall. It was a staggering sight. There were great troughs of food running one whole length of the room, with orderlies in white standing behind them, and long wooden tables for us to sit at. There was roast beef, roast and mashed potatoes, sprouts and mashed swedes and all the trimmings. Fruit pie, jelly and custard to follow. After the diet of macaroni cheese that we had been accustomed to, it seemed like the Ritz – the men certainly get the best of everything!

After I had piled up my plate, I did a hasty reconnaissance, hoping to evade Vlady, and sat down next to a short, white-faced man with straight auburn hair hanging down over slanting blue eyes. He talked to me a lot, and seemed to have a great sense of humour and a truly Elizabethan flow of language.

Gussy got me in a corner afterwards.

'You know who that was, don't you?' she said. 'That's Dizzy Allen, the famous Battle of Britain pilot.'

Apparently Dizzy is an absolute legend in his own time, one of the most daring and famous of 'The Few'. At the moment he's stooging around here on some boring admin job, and drinking like a fish. I took an instant liking to him and enjoyed talking to him very much – something I realised I had missed with the Norwegians. Much as I had enjoyed being with them, there had been very little good stimulating talk.

As for Vlady, he is far too conceited for my liking, and his conversation is limited to sex, flying, and the Polish Corridor, one mention of which is enough to unleash a flood of passionate and largely incomprehensible rhetoric.

After dinner I went back to my quarters. They were in a big hut set among lawns, and I had a very nice little room of my own.

To my surprise I found a young, dark-haired airman making up my fire. He looked vaguely familiar and I suddenly realised it was my old friend from RADA days, Humphrey Lestocq – last seen flinging back a nonchalant scarf as a fighter pilot in *The First of the Few*. And now he was my batman!

We sat by the fire while he polished up my buttons, and had a good old theatrical gossip, just like in the old days. We talked about the Old Vic and Olivier and John Gielgud. We both have the same opinion of John's rather unfortunate legs (particularly in tights) and the way he slinks around flaring his nostrils and snorting with emotion. We also talked nostalgically about the Embankment cafés, the Blue Cockatoo and the Lombard.

I was not on duty until the following night, so went straight to bed and slept like a top.

Woke to a fearful racket, and looked out on to the lawn. A magpie was being absolutely beastly to a wretched toad, pulling his hind leg out like a piece of rubber. I rescued the yelling toad and was surprised to see the magpie hop off in the direction of the cookhouse. Apparently he is our tame mascot.

Breakfast was yet another Lucullan spread, everything delicious apart from the reconstituted scrambled egg which had separated out into yellow blobs sitting in a pool of water. Obviously it's a good idea to get in there early.

Vlady slunk in and settled himself down next to me.

'How would you like to fly this afternoon?' he asked casually – obviously not a type to let the grass grow under his feet. My heart thumped with excitement. I'd never been up in a small plane, so I said I would love to.

We took a bag of apples and went whizzing down to Hucknall where we found a Proctor waiting for us on the runway. It's a small single-engined plane, a two-seater.

We flipped over to a Polish 'drome at Newton where we got a rapturous reception from the all-Polish ground crew, grinning widely as if to say, 'Here's that bloody squadron leader at it again!'

Then we stooged back in brilliant sunshine. Vlady is a wizard pilot and looks very stern and beautiful when he is flying. He has the most terrifically long hair like a Chelsea boy, and a paralysing way of taking his hands off the controls in the middle of a power dive to make a pass at you! It's the first time I've ever had my bottom pinched at 3,000 feet.

Wednesday, 14th March

Still missing Scotland terrifically, and Oscar most of all, though I'm definitely beginning to like it here. Everybody is amazingly friendly, and the work is pretty interesting, particularly when we're plotting the flying bombs coming over.

I've also discovered a piano up at the manor house which nobody uses. I'm allowed to practise as much as I like, which is a great joy and I play every day. This afternoon I was practising Mozart's sonatas when the unflagging Polack turned up in a great state of Central European gloom. He had just heard Churchill's speech on the wireless saying that the Poles in England can never go back to their country. So I played him Chopin nocturnes, more by guess than by God, and with bags of sustained pedal, while he lay collapsed in his armchair overcome with emotion.

In the evening we had a pigeon party up at the manor with some of his Polish friends. Gussy and I plucked and gutted them and they were delicious, roast with garlic stuffing. The table had been laid with silver and crystal but we sat by the fire tearing them to pieces with our hands, gnawing the bones and chucking them into the embers.

Went on duty at midnight. I was on the table when a phone call came through from Scotland. It was Oscar who had been trying to get through to me all evening. She was in a high state of excitement as her posting had finally come through. Now we will all be together again, me, Pandora, Gussy and Oscar.

Friday, 30th March

We had a great day out to celebrate Oscar's arrival, went to the Nottingham Lace Market and ate whelks, ice cream and hot peas with mint out of tin cups. Felt rather sick. Then in the evening went to see wonderful Douggie Byng in a variety show. He wore lady's clothes with a huge bust and sang vulgar songs. He has a way of saying 'For King and country' with the emphasis on the wrong word. It makes it sound very rude indeed!

Oscar says she has heard nothing from Danny, and her new boyfriend is a squadron leader of 42 – married of course!

We have now got concrete plans for after the war. An officer who works here, an old flame of Oscar's, is a staff manager for umpteen branches of Jaegers, and he has promised to get us jobs in the London branch selling clothes.

If this doesn't work out we are going to open a Hamburger Caff. Next year, maybe?

Sunday, 8th April

Veronica writes that she misses me and that the Czech who said he saw her husband has turned out to be a psychopathic liar with a reputation for telling tall stories – poor thing, she is devastated.

18th April

Belsen has been liberated and the first newsreels shown. Everything the abbé told us seems to have been true, only far worse. The pictures are of a kind of hell on earth – skeletons wandering around a barbed-wire enclosure, staggering and bumping into each other like figures in a nightmare. Another skeleton squats on the ground picking at rags. The number of people – most of them Jews – who died in the gas ovens is so staggering that one feels quite numb with shock.

Spent a Benzedrine-ridden night crying for the suffering of the children, and railing against God for allowing such torture.

I've been thinking an awful lot about God lately, and have drunken sessions with Dizzy in the bar – he is also a Catholic though a lapsed one, so he understands.

'How terrible to be God,' he says. 'Imagine having the world on your conscience!'

My mind lately has been in a state of turmoil. I just don't know whether I believe any more or not. It is the first time that doubts have ever entered my mind, but I think I'd rather have an imperfect God than none at all, and no meaning to anything. If children are going to suffer at least let them have a loving breast to fall back upon in the end, not just a cold darkness.

'Oh,' says Dizzy, 'I can see you are a hopeless case – you still really believe in the whole bloodstained farce.'

It's all very well for him, he lost his faith years ago, while my feelings are still in a terrible muddle.

24th April

For the last few weeks there has been a feeling of almost hysterical excitement in the Mess as the Allies score one victory after another. Our lives revolve around news bulletins on the wireless. For the first time we're really beginning to think the end is in sight. We are bombing the hell out of Germany night and day. The whole of the Ruhr is in our hands, with thousands of prisoners, and the Russians are fighting in the suburbs of Berlin.

25th April

Yet another hellish concentration camp, Dachau, has been found – we liberated it yesterday. The Russians and Americans have finally met up on the Elbe and joined forces.

Sunday, 29th April

Today we heard that Mussolini and his mistress Clara had been captured and shot by partisans and their bodies laid out in a public square.

Wednesday, 2nd May

They've announced on Hamburg radio that Hitler is dead! Berlin has surrendered to the Russians.

As soon as we came off watch we all piled into cars and set out for the nearest pub, with Oscar, Pandora and I crammed into Dizzy's car.

When we had drunk so many toasts that we could hardly stand, someone took over the piano and we sang till closing time. The whole pub turned out to shout goodbye. The ride home was a nightmare – we went tearing through the night, whooping and singing, with screeching brakes and screaming horns. Then three times round the WAAF Mess, howling like wolves – according to custom – and when we reached the RAF Mess we found it practically ablaze.

Some types had got hold of 'Fido', the stuff they use to clear fog, and had lit it all over the bars. They were dancing round it, wearing huge negro masks from the Xmas pantomime, and waving broomsticks – a fantastic sight!

We spotted Gussy and Vlady sitting entwined in the dark of the Ladies' Room with a bottle of vodka between them listening to the Warsaw Concerto – all very romantic. Dizzy put on the most hideous mask he could find and jumped on them from behind – terrible screams!

Then the rest of the drunken horde rushed in, somebody got the piano and we did all sorts of crazy dances. Dizzy is a wizard dancer, he leaps all over the floor like a cat. At midnight we all went over to the WAAF Mess for sausages and tea in the kitchen.

Monday, 7th May

Rumours all day that the war in Europe is over, but not until tonight were we finally told – tomorrow is officially VE Day!

I was on watch at the time, and the CO came on to the balcony specially to announce it. It will be a national holiday, so quite a few of us are taking the train to London – I rang Mum to warn her and she nearly broke down over the telephone.

Tuesday, 8th May

We were all of us on the earliest morning train we could take.

A crazy man in our compartment kept insisting that it was all a hoax – the war wasn't over and we were now actually at war with the Russians! It wasn't until the train got in and I heard the first church bells ringing that I finally knew that it was true. Arrived at Nell Gwyn House to find Mummy and Sid already celebrating with a bottle of sherry, in spite of having been up half the night with excitement and a terrible thunderstorm. Roosie, Sid's teddybear, was sitting in his usual cradle with the Union Jack tied to one paw. Outside, the church bells were still ringing like crazy.

It seems that Goebbels and his family have committed suicide but still no sign of Hitler's body. They think he may have died in the Chancellery, black smoke has been reported pouring out of an underground chamber, but so far no one as been able to reach it.

Mama has prepared a celebration lunch from a recipe she's heard on 'The Kitchen Front' – an awful mixture of offal and oatmeal – not a howling success, but the tinned fruit salad was OK, and after it we brought out a long-hoarded bottle of gin.

Kate, who was on her way to 'do' for Mr Houselander down the corridor, came in and joined us, wearing her apron, and we were quite tight and merry by the time we heard that wonderful voice saying 'Advance Britannia! Long live the cause of freedom!' Tears and hugs all round.

Later that evening we decided to brave the West End. Mummy and Sid, who both remembered scenes of rape and wild debauchery from World War I, put on the most unseductive clothes they could find, with heavy, man-proof trousers – everything in fact bar a couple of chastity belts.

There was wild excitement in Trafalgar Square, half London seemed to be floodlit – so much unexpected light was quite unreal. There were people dancing like crazy, jumping in the fountains and climbing lamp-posts, and a dull red glow in the sky from bonfires which reminded us of the Blitz.

Most of the pubs seemed to be running out of booze, so I took them both to the York Minster where red wine was flowing in torrents. Behind the bar was Monsieur Berlemont, his magnificent moustaches practically standing on end with excitement. We sat at the little round corner table, the same table where I first got drunk with Rupert – it seems like a hundred years ago. A French sailor kissed Mummy and changed hats with her, taking her little brown velvet cap and giving her his with a pom-pom on top. Very embarrassed, she hastily rearranged her hair, pulling it over her ears. She never could stand people seeing her ears, although they are perfectly nice ones.

Sid got squiffy on one Pernod – it reminds her of absinthe and her art student days in Paris. She has definitely mellowed a bit and I'm not frightened of her any more.

We were all fairly unsteady by the time we left Soho and headed for Piccadilly, fighting our way slowly through the crowds towards Whitehall, where we had heard Churchill was appearing. Everyone was singing the old sings, 'Roll Out the Barrel', 'Bless 'em All', and 'Tipperary', and dancing in circles. At one point I got whirled away into the dance by a group of Polish airmen and I thought I was lost forever, but managed to keep one eye on the beacon of Sid's bright red hair. As I fought my way back, one of my shoes came off and had to be abandoned.

We linked arms and slowly made our way towards Whitehall – when we got there we were packed in like sardines. Everybody was singing 'Why are we waiting?' and 'We want Winnie' – a few people fainted but suddenly all the floodlights came on, sirens wailed and there he was on the balcony making the V sign, just like on *Pathé Gazette*.

He made a wonderful speech but I don't remember very much of it except for the bit where he said, 'Were we downhearted?' and we all yelled, 'No!' Then we sang 'Land of Hope and Glory' and I think we all cried – I certainly did. It was one of the most exciting moments of my life.

Limped home with my stockings in ribbons, the whole sky ringed with searchlights.

By now we were desperately hungry but alas, there was a note from Kate: 'Dear Madam, Went to do for Mr Houselander after I saw you this morning and he gave me a jug of rabbit stew for your dinner. Looked a bit off, so threw it out – thought I saw it move! So sorry, there's some powdered egg in the larder.' We made some rather nasty omelettes, drank cocoa and went to bed as it was after midnight.

Luckily Sid now has her own room upstairs, so Mama no longer has to climb over her every time she wants to have a pee.

Slept on 'campy' in the bathroom – a wonderful day.

Wednesday, 9th May

Back to Watnall early the next morning as I didn't want to miss out on any of the celebrations, and indeed a Victory Dance was planned for the very next day.

It turned out to be an enormously pukka do, with marvellous flowers, food and decorations. We had floodlights on the lawn and a band.

Even more exciting was the arrival of a new man in the Mess, Kit Latimer, a slim, nervy young pilot with dark hair and brown eyes who used to fly Spitfires until he had a bad crash landing. One side of his face is slightly puckered by burns. It makes his mouth curl up on one side as if he is always smiling but he is very good-looking in spite of it.

I had gone to immense trouble to make myself look nice for the dance, spending hours getting my flaming contact lenses in, and sticking flowers in my hair. Very often I feel myself to be squint-eyed and ungainly, but tonight I felt like the Queen of Sheba. I came down the long staircase very slowly, carrying this precariously created beauty before me like a glass of champagne that I was frightened of spilling.

'What have you done to yourself?' Pandora said, 'You look like a princess!'

The new boy, Kit, was at the bar with Dizzy. They were re-fighting old battles and waving their hands in the air like aeroplanes. As soon as he saw me he stopped being a Spitfire and made a beeline in my direction.

We got marvellously tiddly on rum and peppermint (which tastes like crème de menthe) and danced on the lawn under the floodlights. He was a wicked dancer, doing a very snaky rumba, and knowing the steps of all the vulgar dances like the hokey-cokey and the Lambeth walk.

Vlady, darting furious glances in my direction, danced with a red rose in his hand which he occasionally crushed passionately to his nostrils.

About midnight the band packed up and one of the boys took over the piano. We turned all the lights out and the floor was beautiful like glass under water. Kit and I swooped around to 'My Dreams are Getting Better all the Time'.

At 3.30 Kit drove me out into the country in his car.

He is the most amazing young man I have ever met. We got so interested in each other that we ended up spending the whole night in the car, just snoozing and talking. We lay wrapped in the rug, my head on his shoulder, or his head in my lap, until seven o'clock in the morning, when the larks began to sing and the miners passed us cycling to work – but still not a finger was laid! It was so pleasant and friendly, I was really impressed – but just a bit puzzled. Then, with the morning sun, hangovers arrived, so we drove back to his billet for tea and aspirin.

I like him enormously and I think he likes me, but his conduct both intrigues and infuriates me – not even a goodnight kiss! Perhaps things will be better tomorrow.

Thursday

They weren't. Once more we drove to the country and this time we lay in a field making daisy chains, objects of great interest to a herd of cows who licked our feet with long, rasping tongues – but still no pass. Is something wrong with him?

We drank beer in a very ancient pub called the Old Spot with scrubbed tables and a talking parrot. I saw him wince when I lit a cigarette so I asked about the crash. He said he hadn't been at all frightened of dying, just of the fire, so now I don't smoke when I'm with him.

He has a very nice mind and is not at all blasé. He is interested in things like cows and parrots and the shapes of trees, and he doesn't say 'whack-o' or 'wizard prang' – though he has a slight and regrettable fondness for 'Roger-dodger'!

On the way back the car stuck in a ditch and we walked the five miles back to the Mess hand in hand. It was now 4 a.m. and I was getting desperate.

Maybe he has a mother complex or has suffered some unmentionable deprivation when his plane crashed? Has something been *shot off*? It is very interesting and entirely without precedent.

20th May

Kit away for five days. Washed my hair, played chess, had another go with Dr S's cream – you never know!

Oscar and I discussed Kit's baffling behaviour at great length. Oscar says he sounds just like her brother David who was brought up to believe that nice Jewish boys lose a pint of blood every time they do it.

Anyway, she says, these quiet ones are often the best, once they get going, and perhaps I ought to try making him jealous. I said I'd do my best.

We have now decided we are going to own a Hamburger Caff after the war instead of being Jaeger shop girls.

Wednesday, 23rd May

There has been a great new addition to our social life. We now have a swimming pool! In fact it's only a static water tank, about four and a half feet deep, but it is very warm and surrounded by trees and grass. It gives the WAAF officers a wonderful chance to lie out in their scantiest costumes and be chatted up by the pilots. All around us the camp swarms with German prisoners breaking stones – blond, sulky boys who peer through the bushes and mutter lewd suggestions which luckily we can't understand. I feel really sorry for the poor devils.

Sunday, 27th May

Kit back, so I decided to try out Oscar's advice about jealousy and went to the cinema with Vlady. Saw an awful picture called *Salome, Where She Danced* with Yvonne de Carlo. Let him kiss me. Afterwards played Chopin for him in the Ladies' Room. Kit sat in a corner looking gloomy. Dizzy came in wearing his dressing-gown with a towel round his neck. We did a little ballet together then went off for a midnight swim, Kit trailing miserably behind.

I flirted outrageously with Dizzy and took them both back to the WAAF huts for sausages. Kit squatted on the stove like a Russian peasant with his dressing-gown hanging open and I noticed he had very nice legs.

Dizzy discoursed about God and Mother Earth and metaphysics as is his habit when whizzed. Kit looked sour and one of his legs began to twitch nervously. Dizzy's discourse became wilder and more brilliant, ranging from artificial manure through Chinese jade to the psychology of dreams. Kit muttered something about being tired and took off. I let Dizzy kiss me.

The next morning a strange thing happened. I woke up to find an unidentifiable *cafard* lying in wait for me like a vast cloud of poisonous blue gas. I felt a kind of alienation from my true self.

I thought things over and came to the conclusion that what was wrong with me was TOO MANY MEN. I still pine for Hans, hanker after Hamish, have a crush on Dizzy, find Vlady vaguely attractive, and now I think I am falling in love with Kit! What on earth is the matter with me? Is this normal? People in books usually have one love at a time.

So I conceived the idea of making a clean sweep of all the boys that don't really matter to me which would leave me with my peace of mind.

My father once went to a phoney psychologist called Dr Leahy who had a wonderful method of dealing with these problems. You sort of hypnotise yourself, and when you're nicely under, you exorcise all the things and people you don't want in your life. One of the ways you can tell if you're really under is that your arm or leg rises slowly in the air of its own volition.

Using his methods I set to work. Astounded onlookers on buses would see an arm or a leg slowly ascending skywards while I chanted hypnotically 'This Pole is no good! This Norwegian is no good! Hamish is no good!' Or whatever it was I was Leahying at the time. It worked like a charm.

I Leahyed Hans, who by now is probably married to a nymphomaniac ski champion with 20/20 vision, Hamish, who is pursuing South American heiresses, Dizzy, who is happily married, old Dangerous Moonlight, that damned green-eyed, long-haired Polish wolf, and Petya and Zoltan and Rupert and all the other men who still lurk in my memory and trouble my dreams.

Went to bed early with a mug of Ovaltine, read *The Dark Night of the Soul* and resolved to give up my life of sin. Next morning I went to Mass feeling much more peaceful.

The only person still on my mind was Kit, so when he suggested taking me to the Goose Fair in Nottingham I accepted with alacrity. It was an unforgettable evening. I popped my last two Benzedrine and felt cool all over, strong enough to bend iron bars.

We did absolutely everything, ate whelks, had our fortunes told by Gypsy Sarah, saw the petrified corpse of Jesse James with his throat cut, the African Horror (a moulting old chimp), ducks with four wings, lambs with six ears, and an awful dwarf in a blonde wig called Little Snow White. It was getting dark and Kit was holding my hand. I told him about Dr Leahy and how I'd been getting rid of all the men who had made me unhappy.

'I suppose you've had a hell of a lot of men in the last few years,' he said glumly.

I totted them up and came to the grand total – four. He looked a bit surprised.

'Is that all? Do you mean to say you're not sleeping with Vlady and Dizzy?'

I just gaped at him – how dare he assume that I was some sort of promiscuous tart!

'I'm terribly sorry,' Kit went on. 'I just assumed you slept with everybody – you have that sort of wild, immoral look about you. In fact I've been scared stiff of getting involved with you. I thought you might be some kind of witch who would do me harm.'

I didn't say a word. I just took his face between my hands and kissed it all over, feeling the rough scar-tissue under my lips. He kissed me back and said, 'That's the first time I've kissed anybody since the crash – I was afraid to because of my face being so funny'.

I told him he had a beautiful face and I kissed it again and again, I could feel him trembling all over. We were standing by a big, empty tent, and Kit put his arm around my shoulder and drew me inside, then he kissed me properly for the first time.

There were a couple of spare wooden horses from the merry-go-round flaring their nostrils in one corner, and lots of smelly old sacks on the floor. We made them into a pile and sank down on them, the pungent dust rising around us. He kissed me for ages, much longer than my other boyfriends usually do, and soon I was longing for him to make love to me.

I knew, of course, that ultimately it would be disappointing – there would come a point when I would go dead and nothing would happen – so what happened next was a complete surprise.

He was inside me and kissing my breasts at the same time when I suddenly felt the most extraordinary sensation as if an electric current had been switched on, turning my whole body into a radiant powerhouse of sexual expectation. It was as though someone had mended a fuse in a dark room and all the lights had blazed on. For the first time I felt totally at home inside my own skin – not watching myself any longer from outside, I was really there, relaxed and letting go. My mind went dead, but my body was running away with me, and as our movements became faster and stronger it was like the long ride down from Flichity Inn, freewheeling all the way – look, no hands! – laughing and shouting with surprise and pleasure as I finally relaxed into joy.

Afterwards I lay in a warm languor, with just enough presence of mind to do up my stockings in case somebody should come in.

In the darkness I could just make out the wild rolling eyes of the wooden horses with their long silvery manes and curving scarlet nostrils.

Should I tell him this was the first time I'd enjoyed it, or would that make him big-headed? In the end I decided not to.

We heard voices outside the tent flap – someone lifted it, gave a coarse laugh and let it drop again. Quickly we got up and brushed each other down, then wandered out into the fair again with our arms around each other's waists.

I was in a state of great exhilaration and insisted on trying everything in sight – the roundabouts, the Great Wheel, the Chairoplane, the dodgem cars, and Tarzan's Ride (where you hang on to an overhead cable and go whizzing down like the small change gadget in Tulleys).

Last, and best of all, was the roller-coaster, which was quite terrifying. I hung on to Kit's hand as we hurtled down, seeing the fair all lit up and spread out below me like the rest of my life.

28th May

I told Oscar all about the big O and she was most impressed.

Her new married boyfriend is here on leave and took her to a dance last night but it wasn't much fun. Apparently the only thing he really likes is something called 'gamaroosh' which you do in the back of a car. Oscar says it is pretty boring and you have to be very careful with your teeth, but all men seem to like it. To make matters worse, her beautiful blue satin ballgown got all covered in red Cornish earth from the floor of his car. And – the final insult – he was talking about his wife all the time!

'I bet he doesn't do gamaroosh with *her*,' Oscar said sourly.

Saturday, 2nd June

At long last a letter from Hans – now that I no longer care.

He took the flotilla for two days to Norway, crowds singing the national anthem on the quayside, girls with bouquets to greet him. The only sad news is of poor Danny. His leg never recovered and he is now a cripple. He has been assigned to a staff job in Oslo where he insists on wearing a bowler hat with his uniform and drinking his beer out of it.

Also one from Petya, explaining his long silence. He has finally been called up and is on a petroleum installation in the Arabian desert, poor lamb, working as a supplies clerk. Needless to say, his guts are seething, and his brains boiling even more than usual. But he still thinks I am the loveliest thing he ever knew apart from crystals and butterflies.

Secure in my newfound happiness I wrote them both back cool, chummy letters, and Oscar, Kit and I spent the whole afternoon playing a kind of water netball in the pool, fighting and ducking each other like school kids.

Wednesday, 20th June

My sex life is getting better and better. Kit sneaks into my hut several nights a week now. Sometimes he makes love to me with his leather gloves on which is really wonderful. He seems to have a thing about leather.

The other night I whispered something in his ear which I had read about in *My Life and Loves* by Frank Harris, and Kit said 'Good God! D'you mean to say you've never done it? You and I *are* going to have fun!'

To make life even more exciting I've discovered there is a dog track in Nottingham – I can't imagine why I didn't find it before. My dad had an infallible system, known in the family as Ekers and Spreaders. You eke out your money on certainties and spread it on the rarer combinations. The best spreader of all would be the two outsiders coming in together, but that of course doesn't often happen. I told Gussy about it and she got very excited. Apparently her lover (the CO) is a mad gambler and he wants me to put some money on for him.

Saturday was a boiling hot day and Kit turned up to collect me in what he called his 'cad's outfit' – black and white check jacket, suede shoes and a cap!

We had a lot of fun at the stadium, drinking beer and working out our Ekers and Spreaders system.

We didn't win much at first, until a hurdle race came along, which was only five dogs. This gave me a much better chance. I had an intuition the favourite wouldn't win, so I put an extra big eker on Northern Dancer – an outsider – to come first, with the favourite second.

The dogs hurtled out of the traps in a blur of motion, ears laid back, legs scissoring away while the hare trundled ahead. I nearly screamed myself hoarse when the Dancer got his nose ahead by a whisker. I rushed to the paying-out window. It was a £2 forecast which meant that the CO's fiver had won him £100 – minus, of course, my twenty per cent commission!

I told the good news to Gussy and we arranged for me to hand over the loot to the CO after Church Parade on Sunday.

Sunday, 23rd June

It was my turn to take the parade, marching through the town in front of my 'women' and catching awful glimpses of myself in shop windows, arms flailing, cap on dead straight, bosom suitably inflated.

After we had delivered the Prots to the cathedral we Catholics turned and hoofed it. We were supposed to go to our own church but Dizzy had other ideas, like getting drunk, or letting off fire-crackers and shouting, 'Long live the Pope!'

However, we finally persuaded him to go to St Mary's where he was quite well behaved until the elevation. Everybody's head was bowed in adoration when I felt a tap on my shoulder and a tin hip flask was passed to me. After I had recovered from this sacrilege I took a hefty swig of warm vodka and handed it quickly back.

Unfortunately Squadron Officer Scrope, a devout Roman, surfaced from the elevation a little too early and caught the glint of metal – so now Dizzy and I are up on a fizzer.

This, of course, has put the CO in a quandary. He tried hard to be severe but his eyes were glued to my pockets which he knew to be bulging with the loot from a 50–1 eker. He should have stopped my weekend passes but that would have meant no more dogs on Saturday, so he contented himself with a muttered 'Bad show, Flight Officer Wyndham' and a relatively mild and rather amusing punishment which involved Dizzy and me saluting the flag at dawn for a week.

The flagstaff is on the lawn outside our huts and Dizzy and I stand stiffly to attention trying not to get the giggles.

The CO, however, was terribly pleased with his loot and is going to give me more money to bet with next week.

On watch everything is madly disorganised and not much work gets done. We are on what's called 'Stand Off' – about four hours every other day. So there are a lot of boring parades, post-war training talks and so on. Although technically we are still at war with Japan, the feeling that it is all almost over is very strong.

Now that I'm not doing so many night watches my doctor wants me to cut down on the Benzedrine. He thinks there is a danger of my getting hooked on them – anyway, his last prescription was only for twenty-five and I'm having to eke them out, using them just for parties. They are great for dancing and you can drink as much as you like without getting sloshed.

It will be an awful bind if he stops them altogether. I really love that clear, cool feeling in my head, and the edge of excitement it gives to everything you do. Still, I suppose he's right, you certainly can neither eat nor sleep when you are on them, and you cry a lot.

Kit has a new idea which is to tie me up and beat me with his leather belt – I said not bloody likely, but he just gave me a meaningful smile and said, 'Oh, you'll be surprised, darling. I wouldn't really hurt you and you might even like it!'

Monday, 6th August

It was a sunny evening and a whole gang of us, including Oscar, Pandora, Gussy and myself, were hanging around the wooden gate at the end of the field waiting for some transport to pick us up for the late watch. I remember I was studying some caterpillars, striped in brilliant black and yellow, that were devouring a yellow-petalled ragwort. I was thinking how much I would have appreciated these creatures when I was a child, and how I would have kept them in a cardboard box with holes punched in the top, when I noticed Flight Sergeant Kelly hurrying across the field. First she walked a bit, then she broke into a run and walked again. It seemed odd because she wasn't late for the transport.

When she came up to us she said, 'There's a terrible bomb been dropped on Japan – the worst ever! It's to do with re-directing the energy from the sun, or something. Everybody thinks the Japs will surrender any minute!'

She probably expected a barrage of questions – or even cries of 'Good show!' – but there was nothing, only a shocked silence.

She went on to tell us that it was called an atomic bomb and the whole of Hiroshima had been wiped out and the Japs would certainly sue for peace within the next few days.

I think I was stunned, not so much because of the bomb as at the thought of the war ending. Later, when the meaning finally sank in, I felt the strangest mixture of elation and terror. It was as if my whole world had suddenly come to an end. Five years of security and happy comradeship, the feeling of being needed – and ahead a kind of uncharted wilderness, lonely and frightening.

At the same time there was a small but undeniable feeling of excitement, like the end of school term, the hols looming ahead. I was vividly aware of everything about me, the dusty golden ragwort, the blue sky, even the knots in the wooden gate under my hand.

Four days later

Another terrible bomb has been dropped and the war is over! I feel very little exhilaration and funnily enough nobody else seems to either. There have been no wild parties, hardly any drunken celebrations as there were when Berlin fell. It has all been too quick and too unheroic.

Strangely enough I can't manage to feel much sorrow for the innocent people of Hiroshima and Nagasaki – I think the concentration camps took all my tears and I have no more left.

As for Dizzy, he takes a very detached and cynical view of the whole thing. 'Total destruction of cities is nothing new,' he says. 'The armies who sacked towns in the old days were simply human atom bombs, killing every man, woman and child and leaving not a stone standing. It just took them a bit longer and the men who did it had to be a bit braver, that's all. *Carthago* – or Hiroshima – *delenda est*. What's the difference?'

It's hard to explain but there has actually been a rather depressed feeling in the Mess over these last few days. Not at all like people who have just won a war.

Saturday, 1st September

Chaps have started to be de-mobbed and now at last a kind of euphoria has taken over.

All sorts of exciting questions are whizzing through my brain. 'Where shall I live? What shall I do?'

The first problem has been solved by my mother who has found me a room for £2 a week in Cadogan Street, over Jacques, the tailor. We get £60 gratuity on being de-mobbed and I reckon I can easily turn this into a few hundred by going to the dogs – enough to live on for several years.

Also, we are all agog at the possibility of going to university as post-war students. Oscar thinks she will definitely go to Oxford. I rang up Rupert and told him I wanted to have a look at the town as I know he has friends there. He told me I could stay with a mad painter called Leo and he would arrange for Professor Feldmann to meet me at the station.

'How shall I know him?' I asked.

'Oh,' Rupert cackled, 'you'll know him all right,' but wouldn't tell me any more.

Wednesday, 5th September

OXFORD

Set off for Oxford and was met at the station by Dr Feldmann, a Jewish Professor of Philosophy who is one of the sights of Oxford. He used to be very brilliant but now he has gone a bit round the bend.

He was standing on the platform dressed in fantastic rags, his hair in black greasy spirals, standing up nearly seven inches all over his head. He had a stuffed parrot pinned to the lapel of his coat and was garlanded with dead violets. In one hand he was brandishing a tin of Bournvita, and looked like a cross between the Wandering Jew and Grandfather Drosselmeyer in *The Nutcracker*.

Our progress along the High was a major sensation, as I was very neat in uniform and the result was extremely incongruous. Feldmann hissed continuously between the stumps of his blackened teeth, composing little songs and singing them aloud.

I was beginning to feel rather embarrassed, especially when we were joined by further strange people, a Russian actor called Lamovitch and a decadent old rip known as 'the Onlooker' who has a passion for psychoanalysis. He can nose out the merest ghost of a complex, shouting 'Eh? What?' between questions until you admit to the most frightful perversions.

There was also a shockingly smug young scientist called Broadbridge who kept hissing, 'You know, I find you deeply interesting.' Apparently he is a specialist in clichés, and Lamovitch and I had a bet that he would mention dreaming spires as soon as we climbed to the roof of Christ Church – needless to say he did.

We spent the afternoon exploring old college gardens, libraries and museums and I was deeply impressed by all this oldness, like an American.

Soon we were ready for tea and walnut cake, and Broadbridge kept hissing in my ear, 'Let's get rid of these creeps,' but they insisted on escorting us down the Corn Market, kicking my officer's hat ahead of them like a football.

While we were eating our walnut cake I overheard one waitress saying to another, 'I can't understand it at all, can you, dear? I mean *she* looks nice, doesn't she? I mean she looks *clean!*'

By now I was getting tired of attracting so much attention and asked Feldmann to whisk me off as quickly as possible to Leo's place, where I was staying.

Leo is a very young and thin artist who is supposed to Show Promise. He lives in a garret on sultanas and strong tea, wears a leather coat and cuts his hair with a razor blade – he is also popularly believed to do peculiar things to ducks.

'Where do I sleep?' I asked nervously, looking round the dingy gas-lit attic. 'In there,' said Leo, pointing to a small back cupboard full of canvases with a couple of grubby mattresses laid on the floor.

In the evening we went to hear Professor Joad speak and I have to admit that I thought him a pompous flatulent old windbag. His lecture would have been an insult to an audience of school-children. We escaped with great relief. 'I know a nice café called the Endeavour,' Leo said. 'It's run by a roaring queen called Peter but the food's not bad.'

It was a nice little place, with lots of photographs on the walls of other RQs like Bobby Helpmann. And we had quite a good goulash. Then back to Leo's garret where he made me watery cocoa and I spent a hideous night of discomfort in the cupboard.

The next day was rather better. We had lunch at the Union and saw Jack Buchanan in *The Last of Mrs Cheyney*, which was beautiful.

Feldmann knows a fascinating man called Lord David Cecil, who is very sensitive and interesting and that night he was giving an informal debate on The Novel. We all sat on the floor round the fire while he presided from his armchair, and gave us dry sherry and biscuits.

Then back to Leo's studio where a truly awful party was going on. Warm beer, Bournvita made with water and, of course, lots and lots of sultanas. The talk reminded me of Petya's seminars, so I took refuge in the cupboard and managed to fall asleep.

I had to leave the next day but there was just time for coffee at the Playhouse bar. Intense girls with fringes and hairy legs, and beautiful young men in equally hairy sweaters. I think these women in Oxford must hang weights on their hair at night to eradicate the kinks and achieve the shoulder-length slightly mouse-eaten curtain which seems to be the fashion.

I'm not quite sure whether I would fit in here but perhaps I haven't seen the real Oxford. I'll have to think about it.

Monday, 10th September

Have thought about it. A couple of days later I told my superior officer that I *wouldn't* be going to university. Probably the wrong decision, but I detected a very faint whiff of chains and imprisonment – cosy, intellectual chains, no doubt, but chains none the less and that I couldn't stand.

The sad news is that Dizzy is leaving. Last night he and four other types gave their de-mob party at the Mess. Most of them were wearing bowler hats, but one squadron leader who had just come back from leave turned up whizzed as a bee, carrying his six-month-old son and heir slung in a basket on his back. His hair was tied up with red, white and blue ribbons.

We got very merry on buckets of Pimm's No. 1, and danced with cans of beer on our heads. Speeches were made, saying what a damned fine fellow everybody else was, and what a damned good show it had been to work with them.

At midnight a procession headed by Dizzy set out for the pool. Cars were driven down and the water floodlit by their headlights. The men dived in naked, having first asked permission of the ladies present. I granted it readily in view of my short sight, and slipped away to get into my own bathing costume.

The water was beautifully warm and we jumped and danced

like moths in the light shafts. When I came out all the men seized me and started to dry different parts – an arm or a leg – until I was nearly pulled apart. As I went back to my hut I turned and saw that the de-mobbed men had broken into an office and were beginning to throw all the furniture into the pool. I caught a last glimpse of Dizzy, stark naked, balanced on top of a bobbing desk like Neptune on his chariot. He stood poised there for a moment, one arm up-flung, his tawny hair plastered over his eyes. Then the desk gave a final lurch and toppled him into the water.

Saturday, 15th September

The Mess seems strangely quiet without Dizzy. Kit is still coming to my room and getting keener all the time. The other day he brought a book about a French brothel called *Jours sans Dimanches* with lots of rude pictures, and we looked at it before making love. He also tied me up, and it was absolutely the best thing ever.

Oscar is a bit sour with me nowadays, not just because she is jealous of Kit but also because I am going to live in London instead of coming to Oxford with her. We had to give up the idea of the Hamburger Caff because of meat rationing, which will go on for a long time after the war.

She thinks I'm absolutely crazy not to come to Oxford. In fact I can't really make up my mind and I'm in a great state of worry and turmoil over the whole thing.

One person who is wholeheartedly happy and relieved by the end of the war is my mother. She has packed in her job at the First Aid Post, thrown away her ear plugs and gone off with Sidonie on a pilgrimage to Our Lady of Walsingham.

Sunday, 16th September

Today we had our own Thanksgiving Parade, and afterwards I wrote what could well be a final letter.

Darling Mama,

If you had been in Nottingham today you would have seen a stirring sight. A fine body of women marching down the main street, led by strapping great squadron officers in single file, and bringing up the rear, with a chest-expansion worthy of Peter Arno, your loving daughter! In front went a twenty-piece drum and fife band, complete with mace-swinging drum major. It was our Thanksgiving Parade and never have I enjoyed anything so much. It was the first time I'd ever marched to a band in uniform – so uplifting and exhilarating that I was practically knocking myself out with each swing of the arms.

There was one tricky moment when the brass stopped and the drums continued – oompah, oompah! Stick it up your jumpah! – and the sight of all those magnificent bosoms bouncing in rhythm nearly gave me the giggles, but I managed to get myself under control.

I hope to be up in London soon. Can you get me some whitewash as I might make a start on the room. How did your pilgrimage go off? Aren't you glad the Germans didn't get the atom bomb before us? My goodness, how your poor ears would have flapped then!

Lots of love,
See you soon.
Joan

Kit is as excited about the room as I am. I think he envisages long afternoons of lovemaking, brewing tea and playing our Fats Waller records on the gramophone.

I am a little bit in love with him, I think, but not enough to marry him. The other day I was saying how lovely some children were and he said, 'Don't worry about them, we can make our own.' It's funny, for years I've been wanting like hell to get married, and no one has asked, and now there's a chance the idea terrifies me.

I suppose I saw Hamish as 'castle' life and Hans as 'out-of-door Norwegian' life, both so utterly alien that they would take me out of myself – 'be my salvation', as I thought of it.

But Kit is like me, twenty-four, a Londoner and penniless. It would be almost like marrying a replica of myself – plus mounds and mounds of nappies!

I thought about this, and then I thought of all the things I wanted to do, the strange and beautiful places I've never seen, music I've never heard, books I've never read, new friends, new loves – and of how short life is. It was like a meal at the Shanghai – the awful anxiety of seeing so many delicious things cooling in front of one. Would there be the time, the appetite, the opportunity to taste them all?

I really don't know where to start but I know that I want everything and I want it now, with such an acute and all-consuming appetite that it gives me a dry mouth, a tingling tongue and a pain in the side of my head.

Sunday, 23rd September

A great day, our Battle of Britain parade! We are going to a lovely old cathedral called Southwell Minster to present an RAF standard.

The church was crammed with brass hats and Battle of Britain pilots. There were bishops in purple, a choir in the organ loft, and trumpeters!

We had all spent hours cleaning our shoes, polishing our buttons and fixing our hair and make-up – 'all dolled up like a tallyman's ink bottle', as my old nurse used to say. Made an impressive entrance but rather spoilt it by sitting on my hassock, thus making myself a foot higher than anyone else.

The 'Trumpet Voluntary' split the air, and we were off. It was an assault on the tear ducts that lasted nearly an hour and left us like limp rags.

First came 'And in That Faith They Died', sung to the 'Londonderry Air' – a tune which gets you by the throat at any time – and there wasn't a dry eye in the house.

Then followed dead silence – and from far away in the distance the sound of boots approaching, and finally in came the Guard of

Honour, slow-marching up the aisle with the standard carried at a slant. It came to rest in front of the altar and we all stood up for the National Anthem.

Next it was the bishop's turn, and he gave us a lengthy, emotional speech about 'our brave fighter boys'. Very embarrassing. I caught Kit's eye and he screwed up his face in mock horror.

You might have thought things couldn't have got more fraught, but this was only the beginning. Next came:

> Now the evening brightens in the west
> Now to the weary warriors comes their rest.

The barrage of sniffs had hardly died away before the organ, all stops out, thundered into the RAF march-past, and in the silence that followed the trumpeters in the dome played – would you believe it? – 'The Last Post' and 'Reveille'. Incredibly beautiful, the sound of the trumpets dying away to nothing in the dome far above our heads.

At this point a love of England flooded my bones and I let out a sort of strangled howl. Please, please no more, I begged silently, but we still had the ordeal of being marched out to 'There'll Always be an England', our flushed faces and swollen eyes on full display. As the last notes died away, all our brave fighter boys, headed by Kit, thundered out of the church in the direction of the Saracen's Head.

I think I realised today that I would, quite happily, die for England – something I very rarely feel. Oscar and Pandora were equally devastated and we made straight for the Ladies' Room in the pub. It was crammed with WAAFs repairing their ruined mascara and powdering their noses.

Then I went to the bar and bought myself a large gin and tonic. Kit was already deeply involved with a crowd of fighter boys, all flushed with the afterglow of patriotism, and bent on getting drunk as skunks. He smiled at me across the room and spread his hands apologetically as if to say, 'You see how it is, darling – I'm with the boys now!'

I understood, and went to look for my pals who had found a nice table in a bay window looking out on the garden.

We had lots of G & Ts and compared notes on our reactions — wasn't it wonderful? And how about that moment when . . .? and, Oh my God, weren't you . . .? and so on.

Then we started to talk about what we would do when we were de-mobbed. Pandora will obviously go back to her well-ordered county life. Gussy will probably marry a very rich man and have a house with a swimming pool. I will whitewash my room in Chelsea and then I shall take my £60 gratuity and go to the dogs. Kit will probably ask me to marry him and I will say no. The fear of responsibility now is stronger in me than the desire for safety and stability.

Oscar is going to Oxford — she says it's the opportunity of a lifetime and I am a fool to pass it by — but somehow my instincts are against it. Five years of regimentation — not to mention those ten years at the convent — have left me with a lust for liberty that has to be satisfied, and all I really want now with all my heart is to be let off the leash — to be gloriously, totally and dangerously free.

Joan Wyndham

Love Lessons

Love Lessons is the true, unexpurgated record of a glorious youth, begun in the summer of 1939 when Joan Wyndham was almost seventeen and charting the progress of her colourful education in sex, love and life among Chelsea's Bohemian community of the wartime years.

Strictly brought up by a religious mother, Joan throws off her convent past and girlish ways when she meets a dissolute German sculptor at a party and falls wildly in love with him. He introduces her to a noisy, intoxicating society, far removed from her own, to a world of late nights, loose talk and easy sex, and a raffish community of painters, poets and poseurs among whom her innocence makes her a celebrity.

When the diary draws to its close in May 1942, the mood has changed. London is in ruins, old friends are dead and lovers betrayed. The world in which she came of age has gone for ever, but is wonderfully evoked in this fresh and lively journal.

'*Love Lessons* is a unique evocation of a hectic, desperate era. It bubbles along with the energy and freshness peculiar to adolescent girls, and when it ends the reader is left with a terrible lump in the throat'   *Val Hennessy*

Flamingo

Sarah Ferguson

A Guard Within

'This is a book in which a terrible beauty is born . . . in spite of the almost unendurable aura of loss and loneliness that drifts forlornly across every page . . . To have brought back this trophy from so inhospitable a region is an act of magnificent courage' *Sunday Times*

A Guard Within records with stark passion and clarity the development of Sarah Ferguson's relationship with her psychoanalyst. Written directly to him – and reading almost as an extended love letter – the book reveals how lonely and relentless the struggle to overcome mental suffering can be.

'An astonishing document of suffering, desperation, lostness and determination' *Daily Telegraph*

'As with *The Bell Jar* and *I Never Promised You a Rose Garden*, we are given a glimpse of the hell that can border even the most protected lives' *Washington Post*

Flamingo

Alice Thomas Ellis

Home Life

Rarely, if ever, has the minefield of domestic life been charted as accurately as in Alice Thomas Ellis's *Spectator* column, 'Home Life'. With inimitable wit and perspicacity, she discourses on the vagaries of cats and neighbours, the recalcitrance of washing machines, the problems in getting to Wales and the even greater problems that inevitably await her there – reflections which strike a rueful chord with any harassed home-owner.

'Home Life' has won Alice Thomas Ellis an audience as wide as that for her much-praised novels, and here, in more permanent form, is a year's supply of these addictive articles.

'The funniest anthology I have read in years'   *The Times*

'One of those jewel-like volumes that might have come out of the eighteenth century, to be reprinted today as a classic of precise English, wit and womanly sensibility'
Valerie Grove, *London Standard*

Flamingo

Flamingo

Flamingo is a quality imprint publishing both fiction and non-fiction. Below are some recent titles.

Fiction

- ☐ Sportswriter *Richard Ford* £3.95
- ☐ In Country *Bobbie Anne Mason* £3.50
- ☐ The Gold Tip Pfitzer *Irene Handl* £2.95
- ☐ Ransom *Jay McInerney* £3.50
- ☐ Ice and Fire *Andrea Dworkin* £2.95
- ☐ The Seven Ages *Eva Figes* £3.50
- ☐ Mum & Mr Armitage *Beryl Bainbridge* £2.95
- ☐ The Nuclear Age *Tim O'Brien* £3.95
- ☐ Burning Houses *Andrew Harvey* £3.50
- ☐ White Water *Joyce Raiser Kornblatt* £3.50

Non-fiction

- ☐ Home Life *Alice Thomas Ellis* £2.95
- ☐ A Guard Within *Sarah Ferguson* £3.50
- ☐ Second Class Citizen *Buchi Emecheta* £2.95
- ☐ Love Lessons *Joan Wyndham* £2.95
- ☐ Indian Country *Peter Matthiessen* £3.95
- ☐ Pictures from the Water Trade *John David Morley* £3.50
- ☐ Cappaghglass *Peter Somerville-Large* £3.95

You can buy Flamingo paperbacks at your local bookshop or newsagent. Or you can order them from Fontana Paperbacks, Cash Sales Department, Box 29, Douglas, Isle of Man. Please send a cheque, postal or money order (not currency) worth the purchase price plus 22p per book (or plus 22p per book if outside the UK).

NAME (Block letters) _____

ADDRESS_____

_____

_____